BECOMING AN ANGEL
The Path to Enlightenment

AUTOBIOGRAPHY

BECOMING AN ANGEL
The Path to Enlightenment

AUTOBIOGRAPHY

KAYA

UNIVERSE/CITY MIKAËL
NON-PROFIT ORGANIZATION

UNIVERSE/CITY MIKAËL (UCM)
Non-profit organization
53, Saint-Antoine Street
Sainte-Agathe-des-Monts, QC
Canada J8C 2C4

Email: org@ucm.ca
Websites: www.ucm.ca & www.72angels.com & www.kayadreams.com

To organize a lecture, seminar, or workshop: org@ucm.in

Discover Kaya's webinars on dreams, signs and symbols
org@ucm.ca & www.ucm.ca

Thanks to Shreans Daga, Santhosh Sujir & Haritha Nayak from
Consciousness Engineering Research Foundation (India) for their support.

Translation: Blánaid Rensch
Proofreading: Jonaki Thomas, Rita Haidu
UCM coordinator: Martine Thuillard
Editing and graphics: Christophe Guilloteau, Edith Lacroix
Photography: Anthony Di Benedetto

1st edition: 1st term, 2015
Legal deposit: 1st term, 2015

National Library of Quebec
National Library of Canada
National Library of France
National Library of Ireland

ISBN : 978-2-923654-67-6
Printed in Canada

JOIN US!

All the profits of Kaya's autobiography *BECOMING AN ANGEL, THE PATH TO ENLIGHTENMENT* go to the non-profit organization and foundation, Universe/City Mikaël (UCM) to help diffuse knowledge and understanding of Angels, dreams, signs, symbols, and Angelica Yoga among the generations of today and tomorrow.

You can contribute to Kaya's Angelic Mission and help diffuse and translate this Knowledge into other languages through Kaya's various books, by making a donation, and/or joining our team of hundreds of volunteers from countries all over the world. If you feel that this Angelic Knowledge is important to you, please visit our website **www.ucm.ca**, go to the section entitled *Join us!* and see its various sub-sections, including *Become a volunteer* and *Donation*; or contact us at **org@ucm.ca** if you have resources that can help build a Universe/City Mikaël (UCM) Center in your country.

Heartfelt thanks for your help and goodwill,

UCM Team

PREFACE

From human to angel

Today I can assert with all my soul and conscience that Man's aim in life is to become an angel, to develop his Divine potential and hence explore the infinite possibilities of who we are. Some people say we use only a small part of our consciousness and I completely agree with the fact that we use a mere fraction of our capacities regarding who we really are. My spiritual path and angel testimony will hopefully inspire everyone seeking to open up to the multi-dimensions of conscience and to our capacity and power to travel through time and space. Being in angelic consciousness is absolutely fascinating. At first, however, it is very difficult and overwhelming as much on the physical, emotional and intellectual levels as on the spiritual level. Today I am happy to be able to help all those who wish to discover the angelic path more safely and easily than it was for me, because my research was so intense I could have become lost in it. Symbolic language, which is the language of God, the Angels and the whole Universe, has its well-kept secrets which are discovered gradually, so that, one step at a time, the veil of our unconscious may be removed, thereby allowing our conscience, awareness, knowledge and extra-sensorial, multi-dimensional perceptions to expand. Of course, no spiritual path is easy and they can all be overwhelming because we cannot bring about deep change in ourselves without rebuilding, restructuring our life values and principles. A human being is like a living computer that records memories throughout his life and far beyond it, and these memories install thought and emotional patterns, and create concrete experiences in accordance with what we need to go through, to live, in order to evolve and improve ourselves.

All spiritual paths begin with sensitivity, which first leads us to feel that life is not only a question of matter; life exists to help us become aware that we are here to develop qualities, to become better people. At first this is just a feeling, and so it creates continual doubts within ourselves that cause us to waver between a life that is sometimes too materialistic and one that is sometimes too spiritual, even extremist. The marriage of spirit and matter is one of the ultimate goals of angelic life, and in this book, we will have the opportunity to discover all the meaning and responsibilities this engenders.

Through the various testimonies of my life and angelic experimentations, we will also see that when all our metaphysical senses (clairsentience, clairaudience, clairvoyance) open up to other dimensions, our human experience is completely changed and a new way of living and conceiving the meaning of life on Earth is activated. These initial openings completely transform our concept of what is positive or negative, as well as the way we function. Everyone has dreamed of knowing the future, traveling into the past, and of knowing what we should do in our daily life, but wanting to be right, wanting to be divine in all of our choices and decisions, are essential rules for angelic powers to be activated and to function to their full capacity within us.

What is the first step in order for a human being to accede to and integrate his angelic conscience so that he no longer lives only on our planet, but also consciously and concretely in the multiple Parallel Worlds that exist in the Universe? In my opinion, the first step is to know that we are in fact a spirit existing in a physical body for the sole purpose of developing Divine Qualities, Virtues and Powers. Everything that we experiment and experience serves to help us become a better soul, a better person.

I had the privilege of knowing and experiencing matter and, at the young age of 26, I already knew glory and wealth and all anyone could hope for on the material level. I had built my life and followed the example of my parents' and ancestors' lives as well as the model proposed by society in general. But all that matter, that limited, limiting pattern of sleeping, working, becoming rich and famous didn't make me happy; it created an emptiness in me, a very deep existential lack. I didn't understand why I wasn't satisfied when most people seemed to be happy for me. Without realizing, I was seeking the missing link to connect the terrestrial, earthly experience of our five senses with something much bigger, with much greater aims, objectives, and goals. I was on a deep quest in search of who I was, where I came from, whether God was real or just an illusion of our conscience, of what the meaning of our existence on Earth actually was. I needed to understand that sleep, work, founding and building a family, gaining wealth and glory, everything we do in life has to be carried out with the aim of developing and manifesting Divine Qualities, Virtues and Powers. Living according to Values and Principles that are right for us and others, that is what makes us truly happy. I had to integrate the fact that this experience of concrete life on Earth has to be given a sacred meaning for it to become a true platform for evolution, and not a perpetual wheel of dissatisfaction and search for sensations.

Today I live in a permanent state of angelic consciousness, continually aware of wanting to improve myself, to become a better person. I now know who I am and what I am here to do on Earth.

KAYA

"Being human is not enough… we need to become angels…
we need to develop our capacity to dream and to travel through
meditation in the multidimensions of the Universe. Meditation is
the key to reprogram our soul and to attain spiritual autonomy."

*This book is dedicated to my angel wife Christiane Muller,
my daughter Kasara & my spiritual son Anthony.
They have been a source of love & inspiration for me
during this intense transformation.
Serving Humanity with them is a true blessing.*

*Heartfelt thanks to all Universe/City Mikaël volunteers
and benefactors all over the world who help
broadcast this Teaching.*

KAYA

CHAPTER ONE

THE SHIFT

In this first chapter, Kaya reveals his first steps on his great spiritual path, the first years of his life, as well as the reasons that led him to walk away from fortune and glory, when he was a multi-platinum music artist in Canada. He reveals to us his first deep, overwhelming mystical experiences, through which we learn, and are inspired by, just how powerful an initiatic path can be when Heaven calls us to discover our wings, to our angelic nature.

1. The Golden Blacksmith

Almost twenty years ago, my life changed dramatically when I began receiving very intense dreams. I've been a spiritual person from earliest childhood but, like most people, that spirituality was without any concrete proof, and was based on feelings and abstract understanding or experiences that I only vaguely understood. Between the ages of 7 and 26, I didn't receive any dreams, but I had mystical experiences, perpetual questions, and constantly observed life. My quest for meaning developed through deep receptivity and innate compassion for others. I was naturally a solitary, contemplative person, who spent a lot of time observing life and my environment. My biggest problem was my great sensitivity, which made me hesitant, fragile, ill-at-ease and uncomfortable in society. I didn't know who I was. I was a sponge, absorbing everything, and I copied others trying to become what society wanted me to become. I was *too* nice. I was the one who always said yes, the docile sheep that easily followed, without any trace of aggression. For me, everything was beautiful, and my life, my youth, was essentially problem-free; I have only beautiful memories of it. I had good parents, and I simply followed the flow of life until my great inner changes began. I made my first platinum record at the age of 10, and signed with multinational CBS Records at the age of 18, so from a very young age, through my artistic career, I experienced and lived with a very great sense of responsibility regarding my social role. Being well-known, being famous in my country was a duty for me. I felt that I had to be an example for others. It wasn't a heavy burden for me. On the contrary, it created in me powerful altruism, a natural desire to help and inspire others. I was also a great perfectionist, which wasn't easy to live with, but which led me to continually seek to improve myself. When I realized that the goal or aim of life was to develop qualities and virtues, the perfectionist in me calmed down and set about constructing a logical path of improvement in my conscience.

The years of glory and success were a wonderful *journey* for me, a marvelous experience that I don't regret at all, even though, deep down, I didn't feel that I was a born singer. I had no clear idea of what I could have been, but singing wasn't important for me; it was just my job, and the most important thing for me was to make people happy.

The first dream that set off the changes in my life occurred when I was about 26 years old. One Saturday afternoon, I had a nap and in my sleep I dreamed *that in the sky there was a blacksmith all in gold. He was like an Angel, of indescribable beauty and the Light shining around him was so powerful! It felt as though I had always known him, as if he were my brother come to fetch me. I was standing on Earth, dressed in a brown jacket and trousers, and I looked up at him in the sky. He spoke to me in a deep, respectful, multi-dimensional voice asking, "Are you ready?" I asked him, "Ready for what?" He repeated his question, "Are you ready? We're going to begin all over again." And I replied, "But what are we beginning? I don't understand."* I later understood that through this simple dream, a whole new program was actually being activated in my conscience and in my unconscious, and that it was about to set in motion a fundamental transformation of my life and what I was to become. After this powerful dream, I began to receive 10 to 50 dreams per night. It was so intense – sometimes beautiful dreams announcing a wonderful future, but mostly violent, de-stabilizing nightmares that de-programmed and forged my conscience to discover the memories of my soul and the collective unconscious. Now I know what a blacksmith means in a dream. I can assure you that for years I was hammered and forged into shape in order to gradually integrate new wisdom, new knowledge.

2

This dream completely and totally changed my life. Every night, I studied and purified my conscience, my memories, by visiting all sorts of facets and scenarios of my life and the lives of others. I used to wake up feeling I was no longer the same person. I began to have ups and downs and such unstable moods that I didn't know myself. I'd always been happy, cheerful and enthusiastic about life and the projects I was involved in. At the same time, I was also fascinated by these continual travels, night after night, even though I was sometimes afraid to close my eyes. I prayed for Divine Protection. I wasn't brought up in a particularly religious family. I was virtually the only one who went to church. To comfort and console myself, as well as to ask for help, I used to say the *Our Father* over and over, like a mantra, sometimes for hours on end, sometimes all night long. What I experienced during my nights was so powerful I could easily have ended up at the doctor's or in a psychiatric hospital, but at the same time it was an act of faith for me. I felt it was a sacred act to experience such things. I hadn't read any books on spirituality as I was dyslexic until I was cured to write my first book, so in actual fact, basically all I did was to *read* my dreams each morning, striving to understand them, to discover the lesson in them, to decipher or decode their meaning. One thing was sure, this wasn't all a figment of my imagination because in my dreams I saw and travelled to places and encountered situations that are still completely unknown to me today. For me, it was God speaking to me in dreams, explaining things to me, teaching me, but in the beginning, I didn't understand what was happening to me, I didn't understand what all this information meant. I wrote it all down in my journal, noting down all my dreams, in the hope that one day I would understand them.

2. The End of Fortune and Glory

This inner state, these perpetual travels into the beyond, into other dimensions, although mainly into the heart of my memories, distortions and weaknesses, gradually led me to lose interest in music, fortune and glory. I, who had always sought the meaning of life, found an extraordinary source of symbols in dreams. They were like mathematical equations, and they became more important than anything else. They became my new musical score, because, instead of music, from then on, symbols expressed my moods, my soul-states, my movements of conscience. When I told Vito Luprano, who was then Director of Sony Music Canada (formerly CBS records) and also in charge of Celine Dion's career, that I was giving up music definitively, that I was retiring completely, he was dumbstruck. He didn't understand what was happening to me because he had only just offered to renew my record contract and he had a phenomenal career planned for me. Let me point out that all those people – my managers, my press agents, etc., – were all very good to me. I wasn't leaving because I had problems with them, not at all. I was at the summit of glory in Quebec (Canada). Everything was mapped out for me, and millions of dollars had been invested to continue my international career. I'll always remember what Vito Luprano said to me. He said, "You have money, travel; take a sabbatical year, and when you come back, we'll continue." But deep in my heart, although it was still inexplicable, I knew that I had to move on to something else, that I was being called to a spiritual life. I couldn't share openly with him or anyone else that my angelic life was being activated, but I left that day, telling him it was over… and I never went back to his office.

3. The Rigged TV Show

Now I understand that this change of life had been prepared and programmed in advance for me. I remember a TV show I'd agreed to do 3 years previously. I got out of the limousine and the road was cordoned off by policemen because there were so many people, so many fans waiting for me outside the TV building of *Music Plus*. I had been invited to take part in a one-hour TV special about my life, which had been announced and given wide-scale coverage in the Quebec media. I still remember the moment clearly. I was surrounded by bodyguards as we made our way past the crowd, and when we reached the door, a man spoke to my press agent, saying, "I have to speak to him in private, it's important." "Who are you? Can't you see now's not the time?" replied my agent. We were being pushed from all sides, there were so many people we were having difficulty getting inside. The man explained to him that he was an astrologist and that he was going to talk about me

4

on the Music Plus TV special. "OK," my promotion agent replied, "You've got 3 minutes, and that's all!"

I found myself in a TV dressing room with this astrologist. The man looked at me intently for a long moment, without saying anything. I felt he wasn't at ease, that he was nervous and unsure of what he was going to reveal. He looked at me and said, "I've drawn up your astrological chart and I'm going to talk about it on the TV in a few minutes' time… Do you know that you are spiritual?" I lowered my eyes, not knowing what to say because he had just entered my secret world. From earliest childhood, throughout my entire life, spirituality had been the essence of who I was, but I had never revealed this to anyone, not in any interview, nor even to my parents or friends. I replied with a discreet, "Yes, I know I am." "But you are not just spiritual," the astrologer continued, "You are very, very spiritual. There's nothing but spirituality in your chart. There's nothing about being a musician or a singer. Do you know that?" For the first time in my life, someone had put concrete words on my feelings, on my inner combat, because I can't say I loved music. For me, music was simply a means of communication, nothing more. I told him that I understood what he meant, but he rushed on to say, "But you don't really understand what I'm telling you. Not really, not in any depth… but you soon will. You have a great Mission on Earth. I won't say all that I saw in your chart on the TV interview we're going to do in a few minutes; I'll invent a chart so you'll be protected. Right now, people mustn't know who you are. That will be for later. Don't show anyone your star chart. You could get lost in spirituality before it's time for your opening." My agent knocked on the door at that very moment, calling out that the 3 minutes were up, and that it was time to go; I was due on the set.

4. A Childhood in the Church

What the astrologer had said didn't really impress me, because deep down, I knew he was right, but I didn't yet know what it really and truly meant. When I was barely 5 years old, when I was alone, my favorite game was to put a pencil on the table and sit in silence, concentrating on it, trying to make it move. I could spend 2-3 hours in silence, concentrating on making the pencil move.

No one had shown me how to do this. I just did it all by myself, completely naturally.

From the age of 6, I also spent my childhood in churches. They were the place where I naturally felt best. I was the only one in my family to go there so regularly; my parents only went to church occasionally. Most of the time, as soon as I finished school, I'd head off to the church where I helped do all sorts of tasks. My musical talent had been discovered by a lady in charge of the church choir. She'd been out walking when, in front of my house, she heard a voice, someone was singing. She'd knocked on the door and my mother told her it was her 5-year-old son singing in the bath. The lady was very moved and invited me to sing at the church the following week. In the weeks that followed, I very quickly became the soloist, and serving mass and doing community service filled me with joy and happiness.

At the age of 7, I found myself at the center of major musical events, festivals, and TV programs until, at the age of 9, I was chosen for Michel Berger and Luc Plamondon's rock opera musical, *Starmania*. I was given the role of the extra-terrestrial, a young child who bore the moral of the opera, who conveyed the message that man was becoming lost in his material search for success and renown at all costs, and that there was much more to life than that. I knew well in advance that I would be chosen for the role because two years previously I'd already experienced the possibility of contacting spirits. I had cut out all the letters of the alphabet and placed them in a circle on the table, and using a glass that moved on the table, I asked the spirits questions. I asked what the next mission for my destiny was, and the glass began to move toward letters to spell out the words s-t-a-r-m-a-n-i-a and l-u-c-p-l-a-m-o-n-d-o-n, who was the author of the opera in question. At the time, I had no idea what these words could possibly mean, but when the time came for the audition two years later, I already knew I would be chosen, that this was part of my destiny.

I once greatly surprised my grandmother when I did a seance for her. We learned that her brother, who hadn't come back from Germany after the war, and whom she believed dead, was in fact alive and amnesiac. He was living in Germany, where he had a family, children. We were even given the exact name of the town where he lived, but she was so frightened that she never checked it out. I only ever contacted spirits with innocent intention and love in my heart. I now know that contacting the spirit world can lead to extremely disturbing, negative, haunting experiences because we can sometimes attract and encounter an intensified version of our own negativity, and our dark side can take over our main personality. I truly recommend never to call on spirits like this; there is no guarantee the answers come from a pure spiritual source.

At that time, my sensitivity was such that almost every night I would sleepwalk. And I remember every time it happened. Very often, I stood up in bed and my father would come in to intervene. In my sleep-walking state, *I very often saw myself in an ancient temple, all in stone, a magnificent place that was so real, and I'd see an insect approaching me, wanting to stop me, wanting to catch me.* In actual fact, it was my father coming into my bedroom. Because he was afraid, because he was in an ordinary, horizontal conscience at that moment, and didn't understand what I was going through, I perceived his energy, his fear, in the form of an insect that wanted to catch me.

Quite naturally, I also had a very positive vision of the world, of difficulties, problems, death, etc. For me, it was as though everything that happened, whether positive or negative, constituted events that were evolutive for everyone. Of course, it was impossible for me to explain all this at such a young age. I lived the experiences of my spiritual life in a natural, detached manner, as though they were perfectly normal. I didn't talk about them to anyone. I didn't make a big thing out of them, nor did I feel more important than anyone else.

Once I experienced an intense event in the bank. I must have been about 11 years old. I was a newspaper delivery boy at the time. Although I got home late from shows at the opera 6 nights a week, I myself had decided and asked my father if I could continue to be a newspaper boy. I wanted to live a normal life, even though at that time I already had a private home tutor for my studies since I was at the opera every evening. I used to get home from the theater at about 1am, get to bed at about 2am, and get up again at 5am to deliver newspapers, after which I'd go back to bed.

I loved those mornings when everyone was asleep and I'd pop the morning news into their mailboxes. It fascinated me to think that I could help people, knowing that new ideas would emerge in their heads as they read the newspaper.

I'd gone into the bank to deposit my weekly earnings, and at that very moment there was an armed robbery. I was standing in front of the cashier's counter, and while the robber was taking the money out of the cash drawer, I looked him straight in the eye. He was wearing a black nylon stocking over his head. He was so uncomfortable, so ill-at-ease under my stare, that he pointed his gun at my forehead and screamed at me with all his might to lower my eyes, to stop looking at him! I was in a state of great beatitude; I didn't feel an ounce of fear, and I didn't lower my eyes. After a moment, which probably lasted a good 40 seconds, he took to his heels and ran off frightened. All upset, the people in the bank gathered round to console me. As for me, I kept thinking it wasn't normal for me not to be afraid, not to cry. I kept thinking about this and analyzing myself. I was even given a sip of cognac. It was very special for me to go through this experience. I left the place in intense thought, asking myself on the inside, and even out loud, "Why wasn't I afraid?" I wasn't happy not to be like other people, not to be afraid like the adults had been, and I can still remember this feeling as well as if it had only happened yesterday.

I had another somewhat similar experience when my grandfather died. I tried and tried to cry, forcing myself, hyperventilating to make myself cry so as to be like other people. But what I had experienced with my granfather dwelled within me as one of life's enigmas. My reflection on the first person in my entourage to die was rooted in the depths of my heart, in the depths of my entire being.

5. Grandfather Confides

One of the most important moments at the beginning of my adolescence was when my grandfather invited me to go for a walk with him on my own after midnight mass. It was a magical night as a few snowflakes gently fell from the sky. My grandfather was a very spiritual, interiorized person. He went to church to pray every day but never spoke of his spiritual path. Through his mere presence he was a true sage in our family; surprisingly so, because he spoke very little but always emanated a powerful state of calm. He knew a lot about the world and international events. I often wondered how he knew all he did. He too had had a particular destiny. He'd studied philosophy and religions at University, where he could have become a professor, but afterwards, to everyone's surprise, he retreated to the forest to become a woodcutter, and later a forestry foreman. He had always been an enigma to me, and very often, I'd sit on the steps in his house overlooking the kitchen and sitting room, observing him, studying him in silence. I sensed that when he looked at me there was something different from the way my parents or entourage looked at me. I couldn't explain it but he looked deeply at me, observing me as though he were studying me in secret.

One Christmas night will remain engraved in my heart forever. After midnight mass, he looked directly at me and asked me to walk home with him. I didn't know what was going on because my grandfather had never asked me to walk with him. I remember I was very surprised, while at the same time, it was as though I knew something. I often had these hunches, these intuitions, or premonitions of knowing, but without knowing exactly what it was I knew. The way I functioned when I was young was quite special. I also intuitively knew where I should be. I was always anticipating events and things close to me. After the beautiful midnight mass we had just enjoyed, all the other grandchildren went home with their parents, and I alone walked with him along the snowy path home. I remember well the long silence that reigned between us as we slowly walked along on the sparkling snow. At one point, about halfway home on the ten-minute journey from the church to his house, he began to speak very solemnly. He said, "I'll soon be leaving." I immediately replied with the question, "But where are you going, Granddad?" "I'm going back to Heaven; I'm going to die soon." "Don't say that, Granddad, you're in fine form... You aren't sick, are you? Why go now?" "No, I'm not sick, but my time has come... And you, you have a great Mission to accomplish and I'm going to keep on helping you. I'll watch over you, don't worry." Normally in intense moments like this, people become upset and cry, but to me, it just seemed natural to hear this from him. The maturity I could feel at times like this when a spiritual dimension was involved is inexplicable. Then, Granddad walked on in silence and we didn't speak for the remainder of the walk. Writing this down for you now, I realize that I didn't even mention this to my parents... it was as if it were all a dream, divinatory information that had to be kept veiled. I remember thinking that if I talked about it to my parents, my grandmother (his wife), or to my cousins, they would be ill-at-ease with the fact that he'd only told me. Without too much questioning or mulling over it, without any remorse of conscience, I felt it had to be this way because the others wouldn't understand.

He died, as he had announced, of a heart attack on the following 15th January, i.e. 21 days later. He wasn't ill; he died naturally in his sleep. I remember my inner state when my father announced his death. Once again, I said to myself, 'I should cry now, it's important... that's what people, what human-beings do... I have to cry...' and I kept telling myself this, over and over, until I really did cry. But deep down, I wasn't sad at all. In my soul and conscience, death was already a natural passage into another dimension, and not a punishment, or a terribly serious matter. This inner duality between my own being and my reactions in society was very present in me. I always tried to be like everyone else, to be a normal human-being, to live, act and react like others, while, simultaneously, I'd analyze everything in order to be able to remain right. Oh my! I think those were the most difficult inner states I had before gaining access to Angelic Knowledge, before rediscovering and understanding the way of living, of existing, that I'd already inscribed in my soul and in my memories.

6. Grandfather Guides

I still hadn't told anyone what my grandfather had told me when my grandmother asked my father if I could sing at the funeral. I joyfully accepted. My father still tells people what happened that day when I began to sing. It was a dull, overcast day and we were all gathered in the church for the funeral ceremony. I, who never felt any stress whatsoever when I sang, began to tremble intensely, and when I began to sing, my body felt as though it were slightly raised above the floor. My voice was clear and pure as a Light came through the stained glass window and shone on me, illuminating my whole body. It was so intense that the crowd gave a little gasp in astonishment. The ray of Light shone on me as long as I sang and stopped as soon as I'd finished. Even the priests turned around to see what was happening. After this powerful mystical experience, I knew I could tell my father and close family members that my grandfather had told me about his departure. To my great surprise, this event, which was such an important revelation for me, quickly became a simple anecdote for my family. For me, it was the beginning and continuity of deep reflection on life and death, on the *passageway* or *crossing over*, and the possibility of communicating with people in the afterlife.

As soon as Granddad died, I started talking to him every night for about an hour and a half. Every night I asked him questions and I knew we were in communication when my left ear started to buzz slightly. Together we set up a code, where *yes* was high frequency, and *no* was a lower frequency. Hence I was able to ask him all the questions I wanted to ask and he regularly appeared in my room. These experiences were so real for me that I was in a hurry to go to bed to interiorize and be in contact with him. I communicated with him every single night from the age of 12 to 18. He revealed and helped me validate my choices, my experiences. I talked to him about all I was going through. We conversed every night and he guided me, he led me to think differently. Sometimes he told me, that yes, I should do something because in actual fact I wanted to do it. Then afterwards, we'd talk about it being a negative experience that had been necessary for me because he had respected my freedom of choice, my free will. I never told my mother or father about this. I felt absolutely no need to. I didn't need any validation, nor did I need to justify myself, and I don't know why. I even organized a secret hiding place for myself under the stairs, and throughout my teenage years, I sometimes used to take refuge in there to reflect on the understandings I'd integrated with my grandfather. Today, of course, I understand that I had a program to follow; that I had to construct myself spiritually, learn to meditate, to communicate with the Divine. And I now know that at times it wasn't even my grandfather who was present, but rather the guides from the Parallel Worlds who had taken over, who had set up this system of communication to help me take the right direction, and not get lost during my adolescence. Later on, years later, when my dreams were triggered so intensely, on many occasions, I was able to encounter in dreams the guides who had helped me in my youth. Today, I also know that I was protected because if I'd talked about all this I could have frightened my family, and people might have rejected me, excluded me, and marginalized my earthly, terrestrial experience on the spiritual level. Thus, I was able to grow up nice and slowly without bothering anyone, and I thank Heaven for Its guidance and kind, loving, considerate supervision.

That's why I am so happy today when I see parents who are spiritual, and who are not afraid of their child's *imaginary* friends, who encourage their children to develop their extra-sensorial capacities. I myself was able to accompany my daughter Kasara along this path. Today, she is a healthy, young spiritual woman, capable of marrying spirit and matter well, of receiving her own answers, and of living with her angelic powers on Earth, without any discrepancy. This makes me very, very happy because spiritual autonomy is at the heart of the teachings of my books on the subject of angelic living in our everyday lives.

7. Earthly Stardom

During, and indeed due to, this double terrestrial/spiritual life of mine, I experienced great success in my country. Ever since I'd begun to sing in church, everyone knew me, spoke to me, and showed me their love and affection. In the beginning, it was just in my village, but gradually I became known and liked all over the country. I believe the paradox I was living gave me balance, because music and stardom weren't the only focus of my life. Since my hidden, spiritual, mystical development was animated by a thirst to understand the world in which I was evolving, I continually observed life and people from a very young age. I was permanently self-taught. Quite sincerely, I don't think my parents taught me very much. I would have loved my father to teach me woodwork because he was talented, but he always left me out of his working activities to ensure I wouldn't get hurt. Now, with hindsight, I'm grateful to him because, as I had few friends, mostly just one at a time, I had all that time for contemplation, prayer, time at the church, along with all the normal moments of a child's life that I lived too, of course. But within me an observational, analytical conscience was always present, like a computer continually stocking all of its data. Several times I even had troubling physical experiences in both my childhood and adolescence, when *my bedroom went all cold and electricity entered my head... I saw numbers, equations, data being inscribed in my head amazingly fast; there was so much information that I used to cry out... ahhhhhhhhhhh... and my whole body would shake and tremble.* Phew! It was intense... I still remember it as though it were yesterday, and I wasn't asleep; I was awake, just like during a lucid dream, and the experience was corporal, physical, and very powerful.

I didn't talk much as music spoke for me and created success around me. With the conscience I have today, I realize that I had so much acknowledgement from my family and others that it allowed me to be shy and embarrassed or apparently ill-at-ease and uncomfortable with people without being bothered or put out. It allowed me to dialogue with and question life on the inside. I had created the role of being shy and embarrassed to give me time to be alone, because of what I was experiencing within. I used embarrassed shyness just when I needed to. It was very special but it worked marvelously well for me. Hence I was always autonomous.

At the age of 7, one of my favorite games was to sit on a bus bench for hours watching the people go by, analyzing them, trying to understand why such a person spoke nicely or meanly to his child or dog... why another wore a red hat? Did it mean anything? If you only knew how many questions I asked myself in my life, and even at the age of 7, I was convinced that everything we do, that each and every one of our gestures and acts had deep meaning. Consequently, I sought answers to this deep meaning through all my observation.

A little later during my musical studies at the conservatory, while the lessons on musical literature bothered everyone else, they were a real delight for me because I used to analyze the composer's life and experiences according to the moods, the soul-states, conveyed in his music. It was fascinating and always very revealing. I even did my examinations speaking only of the symbolism, the link between the soul-state conveyed and the musical score. I wasn't at all interested in the history of the composer, dates, and so on. I delved into the study of what I felt and sensed, which was validated and manifested in what I discovered. It was magical, but it also baffled and perplexed my teachers, and more than once I had to explain myself to the head, who was a nun. I told her that the mark I got wasn't important to me; what was important for me was to discover the language of God, the soul states and the workings of our conscience. I remember the first time I told her this, she was so moved that her eyes pearled with tears because she felt my sincerity. With time, the teachers and head were so impressed by the symbolic links I made that they decided to let me continue and even take my examinations according to my method of divine research.

However, most baffling of all was the fact that I looked so ordinary. I wasn't an intellectual, nor was I an inhibited priest or monk. I lived like everyone else and was interested in everything. No one had any idea of how I truly worked, that I had always lived like this, and even if I were famous, I didn't want to live differently, so much so that I actually worked immensely hard. I left home at the age of 15 to do all sorts of jobs to pay for my studies without asking my father for money, or using the money I had earned as a singer. I was experiencing and experimenting life. I worked full time to pay for my studies. I studied full time, but simultaneously I wasn't completely satisfied with my life even though I succeeded in everything I undertook. I felt a sense of continual emptiness inside me... not an emptiness that created discrepancies, but rather the desire to fill it *via* the outer world, until later, at the age of 25, I discovered that this way of being, of living, leads nowhere. This perpetual quest led me to give up my career to become a hermit so as to go even further into everything I had been able to discover till then in order to understand my whole being, all that I was, and who we all are on the angelic level. Becoming an angel is an intense process that requires continual integration of knowledge.

8. Kasara's Arrival

I met the mother of my daughter on a TV set. She was a choreographer and international events producer. An extraordinary woman, a superwoman full of talent and enthusiasm for life. At that time, as a man, I was more feminine than masculine, and as a woman, she was more active, more emissive. Our energies met so we could mutually learn life as a couple on the earthly, terrestrial level. We were young and our successful careers dazzled our entourage. She had even bought her first house at the age of 18 without any financial help from her parents, and like me, she had lived very accelerated stages from youth to adulthood. It was so accelerated that at the age of 18, together we were living a super organized adult life and we had everything and more on the material level than most people might have by the age of 50. Discrepancy between us set in after a few years even if we had moments of marvelous happiness. In most people's eyes we had succeeded in building the American dream, but our souls hadn't sufficiently developed the inner qualities to truly understand this material experience. With the knowledge I gained from this experimentation, I really wouldn't advise parents to let their child become a child star. I realize just how true it is that we all have to go through various stages in order to become collective, social beings, and that it is very easy to get lost in the world of illusion that success in matter creates. Today, with hindsight, I know very well that if we hadn't been immersed in matter so young, and if, in our childhood, we'd had a more spiritual education based on learning qualities and virtues, in all sincerity, the destiny of our young couple could have been different because the mother of my daughter is a beautiful soul, an extraordinary person.

The arrival of our daughter, Kasara, in 1993, was the trigger element of a new program for both of us. Our couple hadn't been going well and, without talking to each other, we both thought that having a child would lead us to another stage and true happiness. For me, this event was wonderful and amazing. After the birth, Kasara's mother very quickly went back to work and my creative work made it easier for me to be more at home with Kasara at that time. My connection with this child was immediate and completely changed my perception of life. From one day to the next, my role as a father inspired my life and soul.

Today, Kasara is the same age as my change because it was her arrival on Earth that propelled me to another stage in my spiritual path and quest for human improvement. Together we began to use telepathy, which was fascinating and so natural for us. I used to study her behavior, all her gestures and actions, her development, and this transported me to very high levels of love and wisdom.

9. The Bodyguard Story

Nearly two years had gone by since the arrival of my daughter, Kasara, and I had just released my 3rd album with Sony Music, including songs such as *The Other Border (L'autre frontière)*, *All Around Me (Autour de moi)*, in a completely different style than that of my teenage success. For the first time, this album revealed my inner spiritual states, states that were so powerful in me that they had begun to overflow. My unease on the social level re-emerged as I revealed certain aspects and questionings I had. However, I also had to weigh my words, I had to choose my musical writing very judiciously to ensure it remained accessible, so as not to scare or frighten people. Until virtually today, this living duality meant I lived in a permanent state of prudence and extreme vigilance. Even when I was traveling and I went through customs between two countries, I was always afraid of being accused, uncovered, revealed, while I had done absolutely nothing concretely wrong to justify such intensity, such fear. For me, revealing my spirituality to people in an ordinary, horizontal conscience meant great *suffering*.

Let's go back to that stage in my life when I released that 3rd album I mentioned earlier, which was the last album I released in French before retiring from the music scene and becoming a hermit. I remember an event where I was nominated as *Most Promising Vocalist* at the Juno Awards in English-speaking Canada. Sony Music was preparing me to become the future male Celine Dion, and I had the same management team and associates as René Angeli (Celine's husband and manager) looking after my career. I was in the limousine with Celine and René as usual when we had events together, and my producer-manager Vito Luprano was furious with me for my evasive, reserved, non-participative attitude. He had introduced me to the world president of Sony, who'd wanted to take me off in his plane, who had wonderful plans for me, and I had retreated into a corner to play the piano to escape from all this intense, worldly, superficial energy. I couldn't bear the false greetings and promises any longer. I was feeling a growing discrepancy, a form of extremism, and all I wanted was to get away from all the media commotion, while still remaining nice and polite because I was never a negative or rebellious artist. That's why Vito didn't understand or know me anymore. And I have to admit that I didn't know myself anymore either. For years, since my earliest childhood, I had nourished a spiritual life and had had deep, mystical experiences, which I had never revealed or talked about. Not even the mother of my daughter knew who I really was and what I was going through, how I lived on the inside, deep within myself. I behaved normally and quietly and politely followed life and did what I had to do.

During that same period when I began to no longer want to pursue this musical career, when I had the inner desire to retire from active, social life, I received a letter from a notary asking me to get in touch with him as soon as possible. Over the phone he told me that I'd been nominated heir to a man who had been one of my bodyguards. This bodyguard had offered his services to my team, and over time had become a regular member of the team during public events. I didn't really know him personally, apart from a few polite conversations and exchanges we'd shared from time to time. I was astonished to hear I was to be his heir. The notary told me that this man had committed suicide. My immediate reaction to the notary was, "But I'm not a relation of his. I don't know him. I cannot accept this inheritance!" The notary then told me that if I didn't accept it, in accordance with the law, it would go to the government of Quebec because the man had been an orphan and had no family at all. He invited me to take some time and think about it before giving my final answer.

I, who was completely detached from matter, I, who, at that moment was in full inner mystical delirium... calling everything into question... my soul-states were in more upheaval and turmoil than ever before... and now this event had turned up in my life! It was a complete enigma and it would take me months and months before I made a decision. The notary called me again and asked me to have a look and see if I had had any correspondence with the man because the will was being contested by friends of his, who didn't want me to receive his fortune. I told myself that this was probably a sign that it wasn't for me and that was fine by me. Because this man had never written to anyone, because no document existed to prove that it was indeed he who had written the will, the notary asked me to check if I hadn't received a letter from him since he had absolutely nothing to prove it. At that time I received thousands of letters every month from fans of my music and I replied to each letter personally (even though the Sony team thought it was too much for me to do so). I still had a closet in my office full of dozens of boxes of letters. I had no desire to find such a letter nor to look for it, but I went along to my office and my assistant Lisa (Kasara's maternal grandmother) was with me. I explained to her that the notary was looking for a letter from the bodyguard, which would prove beyond any doubt that he had indeed written the will leaving his fortune to me. So I opened the closet, sure this would put an end to the whole adventure, and at complete random, I took out a box full of about a hundred letters. Out loud, with my assistant Lisa at my side, I spoke to God saying, "God, if this is right for me, I shall find it now; otherwise, it's not for me." Knowing I was only going to make this gesture once, dedicating it to God with all my soul, I closed my eyes and reached my hand into the middle of the box full to the brim with letters, and I randomly pulled out a single letter. When I opened my eyes, my assistant and I were completely flabbergasted. It was a letter the bodyguard had written to me, which allowed the will to be validated in my favor, thereby allowing me to receive a large inheritance.

10. Sophye Heals

During this same period, we learned that Sophye, Kasara's mother, had brain cancer. This first great ordeal shook our lives and us to the very depths of our being. We had built what most people thought of as the ideal castle, but we were lost in this world of success and material life. Our couple wasn't strong enough to survive this difficult ordeal. Sophye needed time for herself, to reconstruct herself, and of a common accord, we decided to call a halt to our relationship. For days on end, I cried my heart out, all by myself, asking God to help me understand what was happening, why I was losing my family, my wife, my daughter. I had always thought that having done everything right materially, that happiness would come with time, that we would pull through, we would manage, we would succeed. I'd always been kind, considerate, affectionate, present. I was an exemplary father, but that wasn't enough... Our destinies were to take different paths. God had decided this and had confused our consciences. I now know that this whole path was as useful for Sophye as it was for me so we could learn and discover new realities of life. But oh! how difficult the separation, how terrible the guilt. So, without telling her, I started to pray, to pray from a distance, and to visualize her healing. I breathed in, and through love, fused with her in order to absorb her illness; I was ready to die in her stead if God wanted me to; if that was God's Will.

I also felt that God's calling for me to serve had come. It was as if this was a sign for me to retreat, to abandon this life of matter and success. And when Sophye healed *miraculously* as the doctors told her, I knew my life was now prayer, healing, and inner work; that was what God had decided. I kept this a secret, just as I'd always done since childhood, and I turned the page to devote myself entirely to my development and my angelic life. Sophye rapidly met someone else who replaced me in her life, and that confirmed the fact that I now had to spread my wings toward new horizons. With all my soul, I wished her happiness, and I inwardly promised to always look after and watch over her without her knowing.

11. Laughing-stock of the Media

This first experience of miraculous healing with the mother of my daughter led me to wish to devote myself to poor, miserable people in difficulty. I began to attend meetings run by Alcoholics and Drug Addiction Anonymous, and continued to do so for several years, without ever having any problem whatsoever with alcohol or drugs myself. I used to go to the meetings and listen to the people share, and I was moved to the very depths of my soul. It became my new church. Sometimes I helped people financially, sometimes I listened and helped them, healing them secretly through prayer and devotion. I wrote a first book about the subject entitled *L'Équilibre* (Equilibrium), which fast became the laughing-stock of the media, because no one understood this sudden desire of mine to help humanity. No one understood this sudden revelation of my spirituality, when in everyone's opinion, I was just a simple pop singer. I gave interviews to share my change and my spiritual opening, but overnight, from one day to the next, I was no longer in fashion. The entire country rejected me, mocked and scorned me, and that is when I went into retreat. 12 years went by before I gave another interview.

12. Seeking Answers

During this period, for a couple of weeks, I opened my heart to an 84-year-old priest to try and find out if he had access to any hidden Teachings that hadn't been written in the Bible, which would reveal how Jesus had lived with all his dreams, how he had journeyed through his intense spiritual path. I was sure that the Church was hiding the true scriptures from us; that it was keeping Teachings secret just for themselves. The more I opened to him, telling him about my initiatic dreams, the healings I'd done, the more distant I felt him become. I sensed that he didn't understand what I was going through. Although I tried to find out how he had received his calling to serve God, he remained vague and had no concrete answers for me, until one day, he didn't return my call. Then, life set another astrologer on my path, and I wondered if maybe I would be able to better understand what was happening to me. He called me to tell me I had made a mistake with the time, and that he had drawn up my star chart according to the morning hour instead of the evening one, because it corresponded with my program as a singer. When I told him it was indeed the evening hour, he went silent for a few seconds, and then said, "Do you know you are spiritual?" I said I knew that, and he said, "Oh my! We have to talk." Once again, I began to tell him about the 10-50 dreams and nightmares I was having every night. I told him about my initiations in dreams where demons sometimes threw me against the walls while I repeated the *Our Father* over and over. I felt that he understood me, but at the same time, he was afraid for me. He explained great spiritual openings, great spiritual paths and so on, but very quickly I felt that he had reached his limits. He had a really beautiful opening but he couldn't help me.

It's true that it was very intense in the beginning, and that I was also rather extremist in my question-seeking. I remember the early days when I used to sit on a rock in the woods and wait for a sign from God to move from there, to follow the sign. I meditated on the rock and was prepared to stay there for hours, even days if necessary. I'd hear a bird *call* me and I'd run in its direction, stop, meditate, wait for another sign to *speak* to me before continuing, and so on. One night, in a dream, *I saw a highway exit and its number, and in the dream, I felt that I should drive to this highway exit and then head up a mountain nearby.* Wow! I was in seventh heaven; God was actually calling me for real! As soon as I woke up, without having anything to eat or drink, I set out to drive to the mountain, and there I sat, wrapped in my blanket, believing that maybe a flying saucer might come and fetch me, or goodness knew what! I was seeking the spiritual level in concrete reality. It was so important for me to prove beyond any doubt the possibility, the existence of the marriage of the spiritual and the material. I took the highway exit and climbed the mountain deep in prayer with all the conviction of my soul, wanting to serve God on Earth.

People cast strange looks at me. They recognized me, because being famous, my story was in all the newspapers. I was mocked and scorned in all of the comedy programs on all of the radio and television channels in my country. Every week I was the laughing stock on the air, and for years, I was an ideal target for comedians. Today I can understand them with all my heart because it really wasn't easy to understand me since I didn't understand myself. And it is difficult, very difficult indeed, to understand an opening of conscience on the spiritual level when we haven't experienced it ourselves. In the beginning, we can be a bit weird, lack coherency, and be unable to explain what is happening.

To go back to the dream that led me to the mountain in Mont St-Hilaire, once I reached the top, I settled there all by myself in prayer and time passed… time passed, and nothing happened. It began to get cold, nightfall was fast approaching, and I realized that in my thirst for wisdom and answers I hadn't thought to bring along any food or drink. I realized that in my dream, I hadn't been given any measure of time. I began to think that I might be going crazy, that I might have imagined it all. Tears flowed down my cheeks, as with all my soul, I didn't want to doubt God, only myself. During this soul conversation while I quietly cried in silence, I realized that my wish to meet God had been too strong, that my expectations were too high, and that maybe it was only to teach and show me this aspect of myself that God had brought me here to this mountain. Just as this thought began to reassure me, began to give meaning to and make sense of my quest, a bird flew by in concrete reality, brushing against my 3rd eye with its wing. Ah! The joy I felt! It was so powerful! I cried my heart out, apologizing to God for having been too sure of myself, for having expected proof from Him, and I set off home, lighthearted and soul free, having healed a little piece of my ego. From then on, I adjusted my extreme behavior. I focused much more deeply on symbolic meaning to discover and learn how to marry spirit and matter in a truly logical way.

One night, in a dream, *I found myself in the shoes of a homeless person; I had become the homeless vagrant, and I lived wandering around the Earth.* I woke up with all the sensations and feelings of vagrancy, of what life is like for the homeless, and this collective initiation lasted 3 days with more than 50 different dreams per night on this theme. I often integrated themes like this in my dreams. A subject was focused on and I was led to visit and cleanse parts of my own unconscious as well as parts of the collective conscience. Thus I discovered people's different living conditions and extreme suffering, so as to develop compassion and understanding. Today, whenever I speak to a homeless person, I understand him so well, because it's as though his experience is in me, is part of me. Even though I lived through it only virtually in the Parallel Worlds, I know solutions as to how to get back on our feet. Deep in my very cells, I know how long it takes to rebuild ourselves, one step at a time, to reconstruct our self-esteem through prayer, and hence heal the multiple blockages that can create such an ordeal, such deep despair.

Another time, I consulted a medium. Quite frankly, I didn't really need to because I already had so many answers through my own clairvoyance, clairsentience and clairaudience, but like the astrologer at the very beginning, it was helpful to have a spiritual conversation with someone other than myself. I saw this medium several times and I remember that the first time we met, she burst into tears. She cried and cried and cried telling me that I mustn't give up, that, in the future, what I was going through was going to help millions of souls, millions of children on Earth, because they would be inspired by my experience, by my teachings and my angelic initiations. I was very moved because Up Above had really used her to help and encourage me just then – not that I would have given up. No, I don't think I would have given up, but I would have stopped manifesting. I would have plunged into total silence. Coming out of her office, I turned on the radio as usual to hear God's answers and a Quebec singer, Ginette Reno, was singing, "*When everything seems hopeless… when your heart beats more slowly… when faced with war or the death of a child… when you no longer understand… more than ever you have to believe, desperately believe… fighting against windmills, ready to suffer and maybe even die… How can I tell you that I am with you, for better or for worse, don't change that… you may doubt, you may fall, but I will always be there at your side…*" I now experience these magical moments when God speaks to me and guides me at every instant through someone talking about a different subject and unwittingly answering my inner question; a truck going by whose inscription inspires me to take such and such an action; all that and more. That's what living with an angelic conscience is. When we discover this, we can only advance, go further to find out what's next.

I was also sometimes encouraged by revelations and actions that I was to accomplish. Once in a dream, *I was with a male and female guide and they gave me a gift of a golden map of the world. The Taj Mahal was all in diamonds and emeralds. There was also an elephant decorated with precious gems, and many other wonderful, magnificent symbols. But the most important of all these symbolic gifts were the initiatic necklaces just like the one I had made for myself, along with a list of the names of the men and women I would meet all over the world, to whom I'd give an initiatic necklace so they would experience the same initiations as me to become angelic. I was also told that this list had been drawn up more than 300 years previously.* When I woke up, I felt, I sensed in all my cells that this information, this Mission, these symbolic riches were inscribed in me and would create important events, encounters, and life-changes throughout my life. Today, almost 20 years have gone by since this dream, and I now have hundreds of thousands of students throughout the world who are inspired by my books, and I am happy to open the door to angelic living and symbolic language so that they can have their own experience. Even if initiations are difficult, I know what these students will become one day, what wisdom and knowledge they will discover, and how they will participate in the construction of a new way of living by becoming angels, by living on Earth along with their potential and spiritual powers.

CHAPTER TWO

THE PREPARATION

This chapter allows us to experience the sacred initiations and questioning of great beings who are called upon to follow a great spiritual destiny. When we live in a material world where most people base their lives solely on tangible, material things, walking a spiritual path is not easy. Through his deep, unique sharing, Kaya leads us to question the true meaning of our experience in matter, and the goal of our existence on Earth.

13. The Messenger

One of the major events at the origin of my decision to walk away from my career and become a hermit occurred during an encounter that is still one of the most important encounters I have ever had. I've always been involved in humanitarian causes related to various foundations. Today I myself have a foundation that helps broadcast and diffuse Angel work, and in my opinion, it should be considered perfectly normal and natural to give, to help, when we can. From a very young age, I was often called to sick children's or adults' hospital bedsides; and each time these encounters further encouraged my ardent desire to dedicate myself more and more to divine service and devotion. When I am alone with a child in his terminal phase or with a seriously ill patient, I always spend some time talking about God and great existential questions. Since I've never been afraid of death, illness, or disabilities, being with these people always brings me closer to true things, to true conversations.

In 1995, I received a request from the Children's Wish Foundation. A long-suffering 19-year-old cancer patient was in her terminal phase, and she had been told in a dream that she absolutely had to meet me before dying. I was very moved by this request, and the following day I took the first plane available to go and meet her in Sept-Îles, a village in the north of Quebec. The hospital staff and her family had kept my visit a secret until the last minute in case she died before my arrival. She was a very courageous young woman, who had been in remission for several years, and during those years, along with her family, she had been a spokeswoman to help ill people; she had been a shining example, a real torch of hope, love and kindness for the whole community. When I appeared in this beautiful ambassador's hospital doorway, her eyes opened and met mine. Her first reaction was to give a sigh of joy and then to quickly hide herself because she hadn't got her wig on. I retreated for a few minutes to let her mother get her ready, and, in a strong, vibrant voice she herself called me back in, and gently asked the nurses and her family to leave the room.

Tears still well up in my eyes today when I remember this deep encounter. Her first words were, "The Voice told me you'd come before I go... God told me in a dream... Thank you for coming, thank you so much." She immediately admitted that she was not a fan of my music, and that she had been surprised to see who I truly was in a dream. I sat down beside her bed and took her hands in mine to transfer energy to her. Johane's eyes, which she found difficult to keep open, lit up. "What are you doing?" she asked me with a gentle smile, "I feel so good... my tiredness and my heaviness are gone." "I'm transferring energy to you... it will only last a short time." I breathed in and let energy circulate from my left hand toward my right hand, and I filtered her energy field from my left hand to my right. From childhood in fact, I'd become used to doing this when I visited the sick, mostly secretly and at a distance, without holding their hands. I'd never read any books about energy healing, I just did it naturally, and when I couldn't touch the person, I did it from a distance by breathing in the other person's energy to filter it. In the beginning, the first few times, I became very tired and sometimes a little sick, but with time, I strengthened and reinforced myself energetically, and I was able to do it more easily. During this fusional gesture, she looked at me and said, "Talk to me about Him, about God, our Heavenly Father." And so I talked to her about the meaning of life, the reasons why we come here to Earth to experience and experiment matter in a physical body. We talked for almost 2 hours and I explained to her that death is a journey, that the best way to understand what was going to happen was to think of it as entering a dream, only afterwards, she would no longer come back into her body. She asked me if I could intervene so she could have a little more time before dying so that her parents and brother could accept to let

15/12/74   *Johane Chaun*   25/07/95

her go. She knew there wouldn't be any remission this time; her close family were finding this very difficult to accept. I told her that only God could intervene, but that I'd pray for her, that I'd ask if He would agree to let her have a little more time, but at the same time, I explained that it had to be done according to His Will. I also told her that she could visualize my eyes and that I'd send her energy from afar to help her.

When I came out of her room, I met her mother and her young brother and I told them that Johane loved them with all her heart and soul, and that it was now time to let God decide. I'll always remember the look on her young brother's face; he'd just understood that his sister's departure was imminent, that's why I was there.

On the plane back to Montreal, I felt her eyes in my eyes, I felt that her soul was in my body, and I breathed in and sent her energy. When my agent who was seated beside me, and to whom I hadn't said anything at all about what had occurred, was worried to see me weak and feeble, I reassured him that everything was fine. It was completely natural for me to keep my spiritual actions secret and discreet. I continued to help and support Johane for several days.

Two weeks later, she died at about 6pm. However, without my knowing she had died, during the night of her death, she came to visit me in a dream. And once again I received a dream that propelled me even further on my quest for Knowledge and angelic evolution.

I was sitting at a table and Johane was standing in front of me, with both her parents behind her. She thanked me for having gone to see her and said that she'd never forget me, and that all I had told her was true. Then she added, "They are very proud of you here... They have a gift for you." Johane took me by the hand and led me into a dark, empty room. There was a table there, and in the middle of the table, there was a sort of mirror wherein I could see a tunnel of crystal blue Light of inexplicable beauty and power. "It's the tunnel of Light that we see when we die," she told me. "Normally we can't see it until our physical death; you have seen it while still alive. Talk about it, don't be afraid to talk about it; you'll see, They have great plans for you on Earth: a great Mission awaits you." I woke up with blissful tears of joy streaming down my face, inhabited by an indescribable feeling. I sensed that what I had just seen had modified my conscience forever. Five minutes later, I was still in bed, in deep reflection, integrating all that I had just experienced, when the phone rang. It was my agent, the man who had accompanied me to the hospital to see Johane. He told me Johane had died the previous evening at about 6pm, and that the family were grateful for my coming to see her before she died. I was speechless, incapable of sharing the mystical experience I'd just had; I thanked him for phoning to tell me.

14. Life as a Hermit

Meeting Johane and the gift of opening my conscience that she had transmitted became the ultimate proof I needed to do what I had to do next. After this dream, I decided to give up my career, to retreat and devote my life to prayer. Each experience multiplied my questions and reinforced the fact that I wasn't crazy, that what I was in the process of becoming was indeed really true. After turning the page on the musical world, after publishing a first book and becoming a laughing-stock all over the country, the time had now come for me to devote myself to a better understanding of who I was and what my Mission on Earth was. My first idea, that for a long time I'd kept strictly in my thoughts, was that I should become a messenger, a secret angel for heaven, that I would no longer need to manifest, that I would live in all simplicity and do my angel work to help Humanity in my dreams.

After this experience with Johane, my dreams and the teachings that I received continued unabated. At times, I would be superman in my dreams and see myself live and act in a wonderful way to help different people in different places on Earth; at others, I would find myself in virtual worlds full of danger, war, misery, and suffering during the initiations and nightmares that served to strengthen and reinforce me, to help me continue to develop my metaphysical capacities. From one night to the next, I went from good to evil and I used to wake up all confused, lost, perturbed. I developed the knack of remembering my top ten most beautiful dreams or metaphysical experiences in order to rediscover the Light, to regain my self-esteem, because waking up after 30-40 nightmares, my spirit was sometimes exhausted, shaken to the core, seemingly adrift without any *bearings* or reference points, and I no longer knew where or who I was. Sometimes, my dreams and nightmares were so powerful and real that I didn't even know where I was in concrete reality. It could take me from 30 seconds to a minute to figure it out... I'd look at the ceiling, the walls, as all numb I tried to reintegrate my body.

The first conscious out-of-body experience in the middle of the night was quite an experience too. My body began to shake and tremble so intensely in my bed that it raised the bed and all of a sudden...oooh! I soared! *I left my body and saw my physical envelope lying on my bed. The decoration seemed to be virtually identical. I was fully conscious and I was able to think just as I could in everyday life; it was wonderful.* My faith in God was so strong that I always had the reflex to consciously repeat, '*May Your Will be done.*' I was convinced that God was above good and evil, that nothing could harm us unless we had a lesson to understand, a karma to cleanse, or a state of conscience to study. During these out-of-body experiences, I experimented all sorts of atmospheres and ambiances, places and materials. *Once I wanted to fly out of the house but I remained stuck between the ceiling and the outer wall. Half of my body was in the house, the other half, outside. And in my body, I could feel the density of matter, of the ceiling, which vibrated at a different frequency from my physical body.* Then I woke up thinking about this experience, writing it down, and integrating it. Each night became more and more fascinating and interesting. I was thirsty for knowledge; I wanted to understand our world and the Parallel Worlds.

In my life as a hermit, I sometimes spent over 20 hours a day in bed. All I wanted was to dream more, to know more. I didn't go out for days on end. Whenever I had to, I felt such discrepancy between the concrete/physical and inner/metaphysical worlds that when I came back, I had to re-focus, re-center and re-adjust. Sometimes I went to shopping malls to buy a few groceries and I could feel the surroundings with such powerful intensity that at times I had to sit down and close my eyes so as not to fall, faint or lose consciousness, not to get lost in other people's thoughts, emotions, and energy. No one understood me any more; my family was worried as I became more and more isolated and removed from everyday life. This state of mine lasted several years. Today I understand that I went through an intense period of study, purification and re-programming of my conscience on every level of my being. I am happy to be able to talk about it now because it isn't easy to go through so many extremes to discover angelic life and Knowledge. I realize I could have become completely lost but, at the same time, I was an angel pioneer, and I had to clear the path so that it would be easier for others. Surely the first person to do carpentry and saw a plank must have hurt himself, and hence was able to say to the next person, "Be careful not to hurt yourself when you saw a plank." I am aware of the fact that my story will help and inspire people so that they can have a safer, less extreme experience of the Angel path.

15. Receptivity

I loved symbols so much that I spent vitually all of my time thinking about them, trying to work out their meaning. That's what gave me access to the Initiatic School of the Parallel Worlds. I have to admit that I didn't know anything about Jung or Freud at the time, and I hadn't read anything, or very, very little, about dream interpretation. I learned to interpret dreams through meditation and Angel mantras. I realized that the more we meditate, the more receptive we become; the more we think about things, the more we solve them. The first time this happened to me was almost 20 years ago and it was a phenomenal revelation for me. I discovered that the more powerful our intention, the more access we gained to Knowledge. So that's what I did; without knowing what it would create in me, I began asking God and the Angels to explain my dreams to me. I used to repeat a question over and over and over again, for as long as 2-3 hours, for example, "What does a chair symbolize? Please God, teach me what a chair symbolizes, teach me the symbolic meaning of a chair, please." I'd repeat this question for hours on end, and I'd fall asleep repeating this like a mantra, and in my dream, *I'd find myself in a classroom and the teacher would say, "Today, we are going to talk about the symbolism of a chair,"* and *he'd write a detailed definition on the blackboard.* I'd wake up remembering all he had said and write it down in my dream notebook. It was fascinating. *Via* concentration, I had discovered a method, a source code: the intensity of our intention leads us to our goals; the intensity of our intention allows us to enter states of conscience, different worlds, Parallel Worlds.

For a long time, receptivity, which had been both my greatest weakness and my greatest strength, now became the key, the necessary concentration to receive, study, and gain access to the understanding of symbolic language. I also understood the powerful effect of mantras, and their importance. I learned that mantra repetition created concentration. This is how I've continually travelled in the Parallel Worlds to learn about symbols and their meaning. I even use this technique for everything. Each time I have a question for Up Above, I repeat it like a mantra and I have access to an answer that surprises me (it only takes a few seconds now). If I'm not surprised by the answer, it means it comes from me, that my own mind created it, and so I begin again, or I keep repeating my question until I am well connected. Sometimes the answer comes through words; I speak to myself on the inside and my voice changes and different words slip into my voice as I ask God and the Angels for Their help. For example, I ask inwardly, 'Oh God, is it right for me to phone this person? Is it right for me to phone this person? Is it the right time to phone this person? Is it *the light is on,'* and whoops, leaving the alpha waves for a few seconds, I re-emerge with a word or incoherent phrase which always surprises me. Surprised, but also aware that *'the light is on'* wasn't a figment of my imagination; I know that I was indeed connected to *Intersky*, to the Internet of the Parallel Worlds as I call it, and I can then analyze the symbolic meaning once I'm back in my conscience. *The light is on* is easy to understand, but sometimes we may receive a more elaborate answer with multi-dimensional images, sounds, etc., which leads us to very deep understanding of the situations visited. I do this all the time now, with my eyes open or closed; or I open up a book at random and point my finger to a sentence or passage; or I see a signpost that attracts my attention, seeming to *speak* directly to me, and so on. The answer can come in many, many ways through signs and meditation. Living life angelically is absolutely wonderful, and leads us to experience the multidimensions of life in concrete reality, in real time.

Of course, this mantra method must be practiced prudently, in all security. This means that, at first, for very important questions, dreams are more precise. Hence, dream answers are better than signs, which may sometimes stem from our personal needs. Our ego can infiltrate and bias or distort the true answer. That's why, in the beginning, before gaining access to spiritual powers, dreams and meditation essentially serve to cleanse and purify our unconscious, the memories inscribed in our inner computer, in our soul. Knowledge used without purity, with a solely personal, egotistical aim, can really and truly become very confusing. It can mix us up and lead us to illusory well-being that transforms into negative karmic action, or to an ordeal that may be very intense. We have to be very careful with these educational Angelic Forces and always focus on the development of Divine Qualities, Virtues and Powers; never only on the result. Before we can acquire these Powers, we have to accept that experimentation is necessary, that we may, that we will make mistakes. We have to accept that the sole purpose of everything that exists is to help us evolve, to help us grow and expand. If our intention is good, if we seek to become a better person, then our guidance will come in beneficial, less upsetting apprenticeship experiences than if our ego takes over.

16. The First Keys: + and -

One of the first keys to understand and develop an angelic conscience is also to know that everything in the Universe is related to + and − aspects. Each symbol defined in dreams or signs may have a positive or negative tendency. We constantly have to do equations and make choices, which will engender positive or negative experimentations for us, and others. The relationship between + and − leads and connects us to the deep meaning of our evolution, which is to develop qualities and virtues and powers in their purest state. This information is essential for us to be able to analyze the dreams and signs we receive, because dreams and signs constantly define the symbolic variants associated with positive and negative, with good and evil. As a human being, our goal is to solve the enigma of our conscience, to cleanse the memories of our soul so that our vision, our discernment is clear; we can then develop our multi-dimensional discernment, which will lead us to make more and more conscious decisions.

An important Divine Law that we discover in the Parallel Worlds is the Law that *Illusion is educational.* This Law allows each of us to believe we are right, that we act for good, without realizing that very often our actions are far from good, that in actual fact we act in a non-spiritual conscience, for personal, selfish reasons. For the Great Universal Conscience, for God and the Angels, we are like children, and like parents, They compliment and congratulate us, allowing us to feel brave and strong, when very often we haven't yet developed these qualities, but Their encouragement helps us strive to do so. Hence, we advance, and as veil after veil is raised, our apprenticeships are revealed, and we develop our capacity to improve individually and collectively. To feel good in a world that continually navigates through the meanders of injustice and innuendoes, various sub-texts, unspoken assumptions, etc., it is important to understand the very interesting principle of Illusion.

17. The Fundamental Principles of Angel language

In my opinion, symbolic language is the primary key to lead our spirituality out of abstract dynamics and into concrete reality, into our everyday lives, because everything in the Universe is based on mathematics of conscience, which define states of conscience represented by symbols. Dreams are actually codes activating life plans and continually engendering soul-states in us. Through meditation we can even find out what is going on in our conscience, in our inner program. All we have to do is close our eyes and ask the question, "How am I feeling at the moment? What is going on in me? What is my current soul-state? How is my soul feeling at the moment?" We breathe in and out and in again, and when we are used to meditating, symbols very quickly appear. We may see *beautiful horses galloping freely.* This would mean that our vital advancing energy is powerful, that we have beautiful willpower to go ahead, to advance on the collective level, because there wasn't only one horse, but several. We might see *sad, gloomy rain*, so we can be sure that at that moment, we are feeling sad and melancholy. Symbols are active forces, the source codes of how our spirit works, just like the source codes found in computers. + and − are the very basis of computer technology and it is more than fascinating to understand this dimension of who we are because God, in fact, is an immense Living Computer, and we all live within this real, multi-dimensional matrix.

In addition to + and −, the positive and negative aspect, there are also the four elements. These are essential for the study of symbols and the understanding of atmospheres and ambiances, and all the variants of our conscience. The four elements represent the fundamental basis of symbolic language.

THE FOUR ELEMENTS:

FIRE: represents our vital energy, our spirit

AIR: represents the world of our thoughts

WATER: represents our feelings and sentiments

EARTH: represents the world of action

Then there are the **masculine and feminine** principles, which define our masculine and feminine polarities. As souls, we have both polarities. When interpreting dreams, we don't speak in terms of men or women, but rather in terms of polarity, where the masculine is related to our emissivity (the outer world), and the feminine to our receptivity (the inner world). Whenever we see only women in a dream, we are in contact with events and active situations that relate to our inner world, our emotions, our

34

thoughts. When we see only men, then we are in contact with active dynamics on the outer level. When both are present, we see the interaction between the inner and outer levels.

Among the fundamentals of symbolic language, are the different reigns or kingdoms that we have on the inside in the form of conscience. That's why in dreams we see plants, animals, all sorts of scenery and landscapes, etc. They all represent us and let us know who we are, how we function deep down. All in all there are 5 categories of conscience reigns or kingdoms:

THE MINERAL KINGDOM: related to the earth element; it represents the world of our old, former actions, the archeology of our personalities.

THE VEGETABLE KINGDOM: related to our manifest sentiments, emotions, and our sensitivity.

THE ANIMAL KINGDOM: animals represent our needs, and our actions and behavior to fulfill them.

THE HUMAN KINGDOM: defines the experimentation of altruism, individual and collective involvement, as well as the experimentation of expansive intelligence.

THE ANGELIC or DIVINE KINGDOM: corresponds to our greatest aspirations of evolution and human development. It activates in us our capacity to dream, understand symbols and signs, accede to our clairvoyance, clairaudience and clairsentience, as well as our capacity to travel in the physical and metaphysical multi-dimensions of the Universe.

In actual fact, as human beings, we can say that we are all, consciously or unconsciously, connected to the Angelic kingdom. We are all angels in training, here to evolve and discover our true identity, who we really are, as well as the real reason why we are here on Earth.

18. The Scientist

When I'm lecturing, I enjoy making people smile when I tell them we are all research scientists here on Earth seeking our deep, angelic nature. When we stop and think about our lives, we realize that we continually experiment, and we still apply our fathers'/mothers', grandfathers'/grandmothers', ancestors' systems of validation. In our childhood and early youth, we adopt the same behavioral patterns as them. Then as we grow up, we test and transform these patterns, adding new ingredients to improve our lives, our individual and social ways of functioning. Evolution is absolutely fascinating, and we are all an integral part of it. We are perpetually inspired by everyone.

We should also tell ourselves, as scientists do, that in life, there are no errors, only experimentations. Whenever a scientist discovers an experiment hasn't worked, he doesn't hit himself over the head. No, not at all, he accepts this, makes a note of it, and then announces that he has made a great discovery: he has found a way that doesn't work! And hence his budget for the following year is renewed! We too should be happy to learn from our errors.

19. Encounters in the World Above

One evening I went out for a walk with my brother-in-law and my 8-year-old nephew. Skipping and hopping along beside us in the snow, my nephew looked at me and told me he loved extraterrestrials. I smiled at him and said, "You know what? I've already met extraterrestrials. Actually, I've often met them." He looked at me wide-eyed in surprise at my clearly confident declaration. I explained to him that several times in very realistic dreams, *I had been kidnapped by extraterrestrials, and once, I was in their flying saucer, and one of them tied me to a table and very painfully operated on my eyes and ears, and I screamed in pain and fear* and then I woke up in my bed. Sometimes after such dreams, I would wake up and find I was outside in the garden. They were such powerful dreams, and as I understood symbolic language, I knew that when I had the painful extraterrestrial operation dream, I was visiting inner states of mine where I was very harsh on myself on the spiritual level. I so wanted to *see* with my clairvoyance, I so wanted to *hear* with my clairaudience, that I had become unkind to myself, too much of a perfectionist, and that was why I saw extraterrestrials who were unkind to me in a dream.

He looked at me wide-eyed, fascinated by the subject. I went on to share with him that once in another dream, *I found myself sharing a bath with an extraterrestrial that was identical to E.T.* in Spielberg's film. *He was like a brother and together we played and had fun in the water.* This was a beautiful dream that also represented my soul-state at the time. I explained to him that that particular day I'd been cleansing and purifying my multi-dimensional intelligent forces on the level of relationships, because there were two of us, and symbolically speaking, two represents our relationship with another person.

In a dream, we are always all the parts of the dream. All of the places, aspects, weather, colors, etc., and all of the actions and characters represent us. In this case, I was both the extraterrestrial who was kind and humble with humans in spite of all his powers, and I was also the human being who felt fine and was completely at ease, emotionally and physically, totally unafraid of these intelligent forces. It is fascinating to understand that in dreams we are both the victim and the aggressor, the landscape or scenery, as well as the animal(s), plant(s), and all the other elements that constitute the whole, that constitute a state of being, a way of functioning. For example, we could receive a dream that speaks to us of our kindness, and the main symbol would be kind, thereby representing the essence of our type of kindness. However, in that very same dream, there could also be a symbol representing embarrassment, another representing hyperactivity or restraint, and all the symbols together would explain to us the way we experience and experiment our kindness. Understanding all of the symbols present in the dream helps us accelerate our apprenticeship by seeing exactly what we need to change in order to one day express the quality of truly pure, loving kindness.

Transmitting knowledge of symbolic language at an early age leads children to activate their angelic conscience at the beginning of their development. They already have this kind of essence naturally at birth, but they don't have the Knowledge that accompanies the conscious level. Many people have experienced extreme states and written a multitude of books about extraterrestrials and having been kidnapped by them but without understanding the true, metaphysical, symbolic meaning of such experiences; i.e. that, like in a dream where every element is part of ourselves, these people were actually visiting very intelligent multi-dimensional parts of themselves; they were traveling in the multi-dimensions of their own conscience. Of course I believe in intelligent life in another world because I travel there every night now. Furthermore, for me, a deceased person has become an extraterrestrial, quite simply because he no longer lives on Earth, in our dimension, but in another dimension. And I can assure you that the beings and guides in other worlds have no need of flying saucers to travel here! They are always here. They constantly monitor our world, and travel through time and space faster than the speed of Light. But of course flying saucers and extraterrestrials exist too and can enter into contact with us. There isn't only one planet where life is possible. The physical universe we are evolving in is only one universe among thousands of others. Just as we have rockets and spaceships, why should others not have them too? But the Divine Intelligences that govern our Earth and the whole of the Universe are thousands of times more advanced than our technology. I sometimes use computers in the other worlds for complex operations and also to *read* certain programs that have been activated. It is fascinating. We can even put our hand into it. In fact, we can even physically enter the computer and travel. All of this is possible for all of us. The more we activate our angelic powers within ourselves, the more accessible and open such doors become for us. However, it is not easy to obtain a Universal passport. Only qualities, love and wisdom can lead us to multiply our capacities. Otherwise we also multiply our weaknesses, our anger, our desires, our needs. Consequently if we were to visit other people in our dreams, we could cause damage or harm; we could take their lives, their energy, their resources.

20. The Grotto

The following type of dream is classic. I've met many people who have had similar experiences, who go to the origin of their behavior, of their way of functioning, of their very being, in order to change fundamental data therein. This dream is one of a series of dreams I received at the beginning of my spiritual journey. *I was in a very old, ancient grotto (or cavern) and I kept taking seemingly never-ending, really long, wax plugs out of my ears until there were no more.* A simple dream like this, which may seem insignificant when we don't understand symbolic language, actually indicates the beginning of an opening to new receptivity. This is because a grotto is a maternal, mineral principle, related to our old, former actions, and it also represents an archeological, very ancient, tribal dynamic. Consequently, through the grotto symbolism, I was in the process of activating my original receptivity, and hence undergoing an unblocking process so as to be able to hear better, to have access to clairaudience.

I remember how I felt on wakening. It was as though I were re-discovering the world. That day, I went to have lunch with my mother – it was just before my period of intense isolation – and I heard my mother differently. I understood completely new things in what she said. I picked up all sorts of subtleties in her different tones of voice; I could hear her fears, her sorrows. I could have told her so much about herself and what she was experiencing deep down, but I knew she wasn't aware of all this, and my telling her what I perceived in her energy would have deeply disturbed or even hurt her.

When we are able to listen deeply, we can perceive so much in just a simple tone of voice. Most of the time, people hide or veil what they are really thinking or saying. They talk about the weather without realizing that they are always talking about themselves at the same time. A person may say "Oh great, it's raining!" and be happy, whereas another person may say, "Oh no! It's raining again!" and think it's sad and frustrating or oppressive and gloomy. In actual fact, neither person is really talking about the rain. In reality, both are talking about themselves, about their inner selves, their soul-states. Likewise when a person describes a football match that the team he supports lost. Unconsciously, he is talking about his own sorrow at not succeeding, his working all day long in a factory or office, feeling stuck and limited. Listening to his comments, we can hear him express either his repressed intensity or his aggression, his need to run to get out of the impasses he's in, to reach his aims and objectives rapidly so as to win, to succeed in life. Sports are a very good example of the causal link that exists between what we do, what we listen to, what we encourage, and what is deep within us, either positive or negative, depending on the person and what he experiences, because, of course, sport can also be very positive.

I've received numerous dreams similar to my *earplug* dream, where the dreamer extracts worms from his body, removes stickiness or sticky objects from his nose, mouth, eyes, etc., from people all over the world, through emails or in the dreams and questions received and analyzed in the webinars on Angel work and dream, sign, and symbol interpretation that I give each month. For me, concrete technology related to my inner work is a multiplying source of our possibilities to manifest. I love reading and receiving dreams and questions about metaphysics from all over the planet, and hence seeing the activation of people's evolution programs. I myself have had dozens of this type of dream during my years of angelic initiations, and each time, when the dream ended well, my perceptions were refined. If the dream didn't end well, I had to work intensely that day to cleanse the obstructive energies that I had been shown and which, over time, I came to understand very well. We require a lot of humility to journey angelically with dreams and the parallel worlds, that's for sure! They are worlds of great, deep truth.

21. Evil is educational

I think that the most difficult truth to integrate is the understanding that evil is educational, that it serves good. One of the greatest Teachings I received regarding this occurred in the early days of my deep spiritual journey, shortly after leaving the music world and beginning my life anew.

I got all dressed in white, and I also dressed my 2-year-old daughter, Kasara, in a beautiful white dress to go to the church. I'd chosen the biggest church in Montreal, St. Joseph's oratory. I had decided to henceforth devote the rest of my life to God. I parked the car in the church car-park and began to walk up the steps to the church, one at a time, very slowly climbing the *mountain* with Kasara, who was only just learning to walk up steps all by herself. Step by step, in prayer, we climbed that flight of steps leading to the top of the mountain, to the oratory. Once inside the church, I sat down in the front pew and Kasara cheerfully chirped and played quietly around the altar. It was the afternoon and there was almost no one in the huge church. I prayed intensely, consecrating my life to God's service forever. Tears streamed down my cheeks. I had no idea what my life was going to become. In my prayer that lasted more than two hours, I asked God for just one thing: to look after my daughter, to protect her, to ensure nothing happened to her; in exchange I would give Him my life; I would serve Him and fulfill every Mission He entrusted me with. It was a great devotional, mystical moment of dedication and consecration of my life. My heart was wide open to God as I watched my daughter quietly, happily chirp and play in her gleaming white dress on the altar steps. I loved her, as I still do, with all my heart and soul, and I wanted everything to work out well for her. My nights were so intense and violent that I wanted everything to be perfect for her. Once I'd come to this agreed alliance with God, that I'd serve Him in exchange for my daughter's protection, we set off down the mountain to the car.

As soon as we reached the car park, Kasara began to run and she tripped and fell flat on the asphalt. She screamed in pain. I ran to pick her up. She was covered in blood. Blood poured from her nose onto her white dress; it looked as though she had been assassinated. Holding her in my arms, I looked up at the church spire, crying with all my heart and soul too. It felt as though I'd been hit over the head with a baseball bat, so lost did I feel. There I was, heart and soul filled to the brim with my alliance, the promise I'd just made to God in exchange for my daughter's protection, and here she was covered in blood. That night I encountered God in my dream. *He spoke to me in a powerful voice, saying, "You want me to protect her, to keep her in a bubble, is that what you want? You want to prevent her from learning, from experimenting, do you? Don't you know that a virus can reinforce the immune system? You need to understand that evil, wrong-doing, what hurts, is educational."* I didn't go back to sleep, I knelt down by my bedside and apologized to God with all my heart, thanking Him with all my soul for coming to speak to me, to teach me. I was so moved! The following nights, I continued to receive other powerful dreams helping me discover the deep, deep meaning of this Divine Law that He had just taught me. Since then, the concept that *evil is educational* has become one of the keystones of my faith and understanding of the world. It made so much sense and explained the inexplicable, the apparent injustices we encounter in our daily lives.

22. Meeting King Solomon

Another great encounter was my meeting King Solomon. It was 7am when I woke up from this dream.

I was standing in front of the Ark of the Covenant in an ancient temple in ancient Jerusalem. Everything was so real and majestic. Standing there in front of me was King Solomon all dressed in clothes richly decorated with precious gems and diamonds. He had a long white beard and he emanated such nobility, such wisdom! On his right, there was an Eygptian princess, all dressed in white decorated with precious gems too. On his left, there was a Jewish princess; she too was dressed in white clothes decorated with glowing, sparkling gems. All three of them were perfect and magnificent. King Solomon was getting ready to marry them but I didn't see their future husbands, only the two princesses. Just then, I heard the Voice of God telling me to solve the enigma of the Star of David."

As soon as I woke up, I wanted to solve the enigma straightaway. I immediately set off in the car to the nearest church to find a Bible to read all the passages about King Solomon. Since I didn't come from a particularly religious family, I only had a vague idea of his story, and I ardently wanted to understand my dream. On arrival at the church at 7.15am, I found it closed, and I had to wait till 10am for the bookstore in my village to open up before I could find a Bible. In the bookstore, I discreetly looked for more information about King Solomon, the Star of David, and the Ark of the Covenant. On seeing me consult so many books, the owner of the store must have felt a lot of compassion for me. Recognizing me, knowing that stories describing me as the crazy man in the village had been splashed all over the newspapers and magazines, he very gently came up to me and said, "I know a Swiss lady who just recently immigrated to this region. She knows symbols. Maybe she could help you. If you wish, you can leave me your telephone number, and if she agrees, she could call you." I thanked him for his kindness and left him my number.

Christiane, who, two years later, would become my wife, called me the following day. Her voice was so comforting and consoling! I, who had been rejected by everyone, and who could so easily, intuitively, decode tonalities symbolically, I knew that this was the first time in my entire life that I had heard such a true voice, a voice with such depth.

23. Beginning Angel Work

This was how I came in contact with Angel work for the first time. Christiane, who had already been studying angelic states of conscience for several years, was getting ready to give her first lecture on the subject in this region. It was a lecture on accompanying people in their terminal phase with the help of Angel work. From our very first encounter, I had exactly the same feeling as when I met the Golden Blacksmith. She was as radiant as the sun, and she reassured me, telling me that she too had been through several years of initiations, intense highs and lows, with powerful, revealing nightmares. She gave me several keys to symbols, but she admitted that what I was going through was unique; she had never heard of such an intense spiritual journey. She told me that I was following in the footsteps of the great initiates who went through searing ordeals to transform themselves and accede to Knowledge. Oh! How I enjoyed opening my heart and talking with her! I revealed myself, and I felt that instead of feeling afraid, she admired what I was going through. This was so new for me. I had been alone with all these questions and answers, all these secrets, all these undisclosed Teachings. I was very moved when she said, "You know, none of the great initiates were understood; they were all rejected by their families and friends, by their nations. They crossed endless deserts." And her mere presence encouraged and inspired me more than what she could teach me. She emanated such wonderful, magnificent energy of love and wisdom, I felt reassured, listened to, and understood for the first time in my life.

She explained to me that the Angels and Archangels weren't people or beings, but States of Divine Conscience that represent God's qualities, virtues and powers in their purest Heavenly state. Each Angel Name is in Hebrew and has a specific meaning; e.g. Mikaël means *Like God*; Gabriel, *God's purity*. She explained that as human beings, our work was to experiment the Angel's forces, strengths, and qualities in order to integrate them, to activate our divinity and become angels on Earth. She told me that the image of a human being with wings was a metaphor, expressing our potential as human beings to embody and become these Heavenly forces and powers. She revealed to me that an angel was an ideal symbol to represent a dreamer, a person who travels in the multi-dimensions of the Universe, who has clairvoyance, clairaudience, and clairsentience. These words resonated in me as ever so natural, evident, real, true Knowledge. She also explained to me the origins of the Angels and Archangels. There wasn't only Mikaël, Gabriel, and Raphaël, but in fact, at the origin of Angels and Archangels, there were 72 Angels and 10 Archangels, and we could use these sacred Names and Forces, repeating them like mantras. This would trigger dreams in us, render them more structured, and hence our dreams would become multi-dimensional teaching and guidance. This was completely logical to me, as I'd already been doing this when talking to God with my question mantras so that He could teach me His symbolic language in my dreams. Yes indeed, a winged Angel was a symbol of the dreamer, of a human being who has access to his divine nature.

It only took one encounter with Christiane for me to start working with the 72 Angels. In the beginning, I started invoking all 72 at the same time. Within three weeks, I already knew them off by heart. I repeated these Sacred Names over and over and over again: *Vehuiah, Jeliel, Sitael, Elemiah, Mahasiah, Lelahel, Achaiah, Cahetel, etc.* And wow! I received dreams about nuclear bombs, earthquakes, erupting volcanoes. Now, with the Angels, I was better able to understand the apocalypse texts in the Bible, which don't explain the end of the world, but rather the end of *a* world, a world within ourselves, the end of non-spiritual, ordinary conscience, and the beginning of our human mutation toward the divine, toward divinity, toward angelic living. Everything became clear in my head. The Seals of the Apocalypse were in fact openings of conscience, purifications, cleansing of negative, destructive forces, such as those we encounter in nightmares. I shared my discoveries and joy with my friend, Christiane. We met regularly, and she also gave me angelic energy treatments. It was such a great help to receive energy of unconditional love and wisdom. At the same time, Christiane was also amazed to see me advance so quickly with the Angels. It was as though I'd always known this Teaching. She helped me realize that it might be wiser to invoke one Angel at a time. I think she wanted to make sure I didn't explode! I followed her advice and indeed, it was better; just as powerful, but much more precise. I realized that through Angel invocation, all my dreams represented the Angelic State of Conscience I was working with. All the beautiful dreams reflected the qualities, and all the nightmares reflected the human distortions.

Here is an example of what an Angel represents:

ANGEL 8 CAHETEL

* Divine Blessing
* Gratitude
* Materializes God's Will
* Conceiving, giving birth
* Easy success, progress, helps to change one's lifestyle
* Great capacity for work, active life
* Material wealth
* Fertile lands, abundant harvests, food for the soul
* In harmony with the Cosmic Laws
* Patron of the four elements: fire, air, water, earth
*Sets us free from evil spirits

Human distortions related to Angel 8 Cahetel

• *Self-interest, self-centered, predator*
• *Material failure, ruin*
• *Useless, sterile activities*
• *Excessive willfulness, rigidity*
• *Tyranny, pride, bad-temper, blasphemy*
• *Wealth used solely for material purpose*
• *Torrential rains, floods, polluted waters*
• *Catastrophic climate, fires*
• *Confused feelings, aggression, transgression*
• *Corruption, defies the law, crushes others*

Hence, working with the 72 Angels, using Angel mantras, one Angel at a time, following the Angel Calendar that defines each Angel reigning over a 5-day period, I began to experience a more concrete spiritual path, where I received more precise answers. The mantra or Angel recitation is very easy to do. We simply repeat the Name of an Angel as often as possible. For example: *Cahetel, Cahetel, Cahetel, Cahetel, Cahetel, Cahetel, Cahetel, Cahetel, Cahetel, Cahetel, Cahetel, Cahetel, Cahetel,* and so on. The Angel becomes like a map of our individual and collective unconscious, and allows us to travel in the multi-dimensions in all security. If we don't already dream, or remember our dreams, It activates them, and answers our questions, because all of the dreams and signs we receive can be validated and identified with the field of Angelic conscience we are working with. Hence we can find the theme of our beautiful dreams in the qualities, and our nightmares in the human distortions. For example, while invoking Angel Cahetel, we might receive a dream showing material success or difficulties achieving our goals, etc. This work is simple, but truly very, very powerful, I can assure you of that since I've been doing it for almost 20 years. What is wonderful is that I still communicate directly with God, and also through the Angels because They represent His Qualities and Divine Forces. Thus my spiritual path is now more concrete and less abstract because the Teachings can always be referred to the Angelic Essence I'm working with. Like a scientist, I regularly wake up during the night and write down the answers and Teachings I receive to continue my evolution, and to help others embody angelic conscience.

24. Bitten by Demons

And so accompanied by Angel work with the 72 Angels, I retreated from the world and became a hermit in order to complete this phase of angelic evolution. I now had the keys to the Universe to continue the opening of my conscience and discovery of the Parallel Worlds. This work, which had been set in motion several years previously, since earliest childhood in fact, continued to progress even though it was sometimes very difficult. My fascination with the Angels was now concrete. Now I had the tools to purify myself, to completely transform myself, and my ultimate goal was to become angelic, i.e. to serve Heaven here on Earth.

Invoking Angels daily gradually led me to visit different facets of my personal and universal conscience. My evolution continued to intensify at top speed. Initiations took on a new dimension because everything became more intense, more powerful, and more collective. The fact that every day I invoked the Name of an Angel, representing Divine Forces of elevation, of evolution, led to my dreams being more and more detailed. They became like films, multi-dimensional, sensorial experiences, extraordinary learning experiences, amazing apprenticeships.

Shortly after I began doing Angel recitation, I had a powerful, troubling experience. And I feel it is right to share it with you now, not to impress you, no, but so that if it ever happens to you, you'll know what to do, you'll know not to panic, because evil is always educational. No matter how strong and powerful evil may be, it only ever serves good. It exists to test us, to reinforce and strengthen us so that the Warrior of Light that exists in all of us may emerge. In lectures now, I often compare initiatic training with military training. Soldiers are often humiliated and subjected to insults with the sole aim of shattering their ego, as well as their willpower, to ensure they do not use their strength, force, or weapon in personal circumstances, or for revenge, but only to serve good in cases of absolute necessity. Initiatic combats to integrate angelic living are similar because the divine powers and forces we are in the process of developing are so powerful that they have to be continually tested and purified so that we never use them for our personal needs. They are continually tested and purified to ensure we never ever use them solely for personal reasons, or to nourish our ego and obtain privileges that are harmful to others. You think military training is difficult! You haven't seen anything yet because let me tell you, Angel training, i.e. training to develop qualities and virtues, to be kind, right, and honest at all times, in all circumstances, here on Earth as well as in the Parallel Worlds, is quite an exploit. That's why angelic training practice is so intense.

The aim of invoking Angels is always to develop and embody Divine Qualities, to one day become them. However, to discover qualitative powers, we have to cleanse our weaknesses and distortions of those same powers. To achieve our aim, we go through multiple initiations, which can be very de-structuring. Everyone needs to know – and my wife Christiane and I talk about it in our books, including *The Book of Angels, The Hidden Secrets* – that true Angel work has nothing whatsoever to do with *La-La Land*. Angel work is sometimes presented much too lightly, in an airy-fairy, poetic way, whereas in actual fact original Angel work, which comes from the Christian, Jewish, and Muslim traditions, is very intense work on reprogramming and developing our conscience. This age-old, traditional heritage and knowledge is compatible and accessible to each and every one of us regardless of our religion or philosophy. Angels are universal symbols representing man's highest aspirations. They are Forces that exist within us whether we are aware of them or not.

At the beginning of my spiritual path with Angel Recitation, I invoked Angel Haamiah, whose Qualities are related to:

* **Sense of ritual and preparation**
* **Leads to the highest, utmost human achievements and realizations**
* **High place of transcendence**
* **Exorcism, dissolves inner and outer violence**
* **Rituals, ceremonies, initiations**

When distorted by human beings, aggression, violence, demonic, evil spirit, possession, etc., are engendered.

During the night, I had a dream wherein *I was paralyzed in bed by an evil force; I could no longer move nor cry out, and I felt as though black substances were entering my veins.* I woke up and this dream, these feelings, my paralysis were still present in my physical body as though the dream hadn't ended. I started to invoke "*Haamiah, Haamiah, Haamiah...*" and in my bedroom, I actually heard a demonic voice say, "But you are not this Force; you haven't got this Power. You are not yet this Angel, and you never will be. I'm going to do all I can to prevent you." And he bit my toe to enter my body. I felt the demon take possession of my body and I kept on praying and invoking "*Haamiah, Haamiah...*" with love in my heart so as to exorcise it out of myself, and finally, the demon came out of my throat while I screamed in pain. When I got up, I actually had bite marks on my big toe and on my neck that remained visible for a few days, before disappearing completely. As difficult and negative as this dream may appear to be, it gave me even more courage to persevere in developing Angelic Qualities since it was proof that the more I strengthened and reinforced myself, the closer I came to achieving my ultimate goal. I've always remembered what the demon told me, "I'm going to do all I can to prevent you." Those words didn't frighten me. For me, they confirmed the fact that demons were forces that served Good, that like a demanding, *barking* army captain, their role was to train us to embody Good and not react negatively to violence, insults or any other form of evil.

25. Encountering My Dark Side

Another fascinating initiatic event was one where I encountered my dark side. *I met my double in a dream... there was me and I could see my negative double. I spoke to him and gently told him that he had to change because I was going to spend my life praying and working for him to become a positive force. I could feel so much meanness emanating from this double. I was even aware of looking at him, studying him, and reflecting on what he was* and when I woke up, I was so happy to have seen him. At the same time, this encounter plunged me into deep reflection on the negative forces that we all have within ourselves. I felt that this dark side had a capacity to commit acts that I would never have consciously thought myself capable of committing. This led me to think about criminals and those people who become their dark side. In actual fact, we all have doses of darkness within us, but the difference between a criminal and a non-criminal is a question of how concentrated the dosage is. A criminal has over 60% negativity, whereas a more stable person may have 35-40%, which means that good is sufficiently strong and so can prevent his darker personality, thoughts, and forces from taking over.

Through prayer and setting new actions, behavior and attitudes in motion, the worst criminal can rebuild himself, reconstruct his conscience, lower his level of negativity, and hence restore the balance of good in his conscience. In fact, lowering the percentage of negativity in us until one day there is no longer any at all is everyone's goal. We all aim to serve good at all times, in all circumstances. However, to do so, many experimentations, choices, and temptations occur as tests so that we can gradually reach this stage of transcendence of our personal and collective negativity. Of course it is work that takes a long time. Eternal life is long. In fact, eternal life means that even after this life, we continue to evolve, learn and transform ourselves, in one form or another.

26. The Pencil Story

One day, in a dream, *I was in a car with a guide from the Parallel Worlds. He was driving and we advanced together. As he was driving along, he handed me a pencil and said, "Drink this. You are going to go through an initiation where you will discover and experience alcoholism. It is intense. You are going to see what people who become disheartened and lose their courage go through." I took the pencil from him, and he said, "Are you ready?" I replied submissively and respectfully, like one of God's good soldiers, "Yes, I'm ready." And I drank the pencil as though it were a glass of water.* Instantaneously, I woke up and I felt heavy. My head was all confused and I hadn't the slightest desire to get out of bed. My vision was limited to my suffering as though there was nothing else that mattered in the world. I, who had never drunk much alcohol, apart from a few occasions when I'd tried it out, found myself in another body, in another life. Even though this initiation occurred almost 16 years ago, I remember the physical and inner sensations like it was yesterday. I can still see myself crawling up the stairs, crying, sobbing, feeling utterly miserable. I no longer had any self-esteem. I was drowning in despair. I had managed to crawl to the phone and call my friend Christiane (who was later to become my wife) to come and help me. It was so intense. I was nothing but a hopeless, human wreck. I was living in such a deep, deep abyss of despair. This initiation lasted three days: Friday, Saturday, Sunday. I was living a nightmare, seeing all sorts of experiences, scenarios of sadness, lies, hiding, and shame, mingled with a need to forget, to flee, to project a happy self-image in places with people who seemed to be friends, but whose friendship was only based on appearances and a need for love and attention. Christiane came to my rescue and helped me back into bed. Occasionally, as a safety precaution, when things became unbearable, or when I didn't know what was going to happen to me, I used to call her and talk, or ask her to come by when I felt I might be in serious danger. I didn't believe anything would really happen to me, but I preferred to take precautions just in case. Christiane was sometimes afraid of what could happen, but she put her trust in God and considered me a pioneer, clearing pathways, preparing the ground for others; a pioneer who one day would be able to tell the world what he had become and how. She had such faith in me. All I wanted was to get ever closer to the Light, and I was so concentrated in my hermit's quest that love for a woman no longer seemed necessary or possible in my life. I had programmed myself to become a kind of monk, believing that ultimately this was the one and only way to serve God on the highest level. At that time, I was convinced that my path was to live alone in prayer and angelic service. Much later, I learned in dreams that Christiane was destined to be my wife. I was convinced that the first dream I received about this was another test. It took several more dreams to convince me that I too had a right to love and to be loved, and that what I would live in a spiritual, angelic couple would raise me higher than I could have imagined at the time.

During those intense initiations that lasted months and years, even in the most painful moments, in my deepest suffering and anguish, there was one thing that never left me, one *light* or *fire* that was never extinguished, and that was my faith in God and the 72 Angelic States of Conscience. I continued to pray, to invoke an Angel. Sometimes my invocation was little more that a whispered breath or sound; and sometimes, when my conscience slowed down, it was soundless, silent, only on the inside. At times I didn't feel anything anymore. It was as if I'd been completely disconnected from the Divine Source, but I persevered, praying non-stop to purify myself and become a better soul.

CHAPTER THREE
THE AWAKENING

The Awakening is another fascinating chapter where the author, shows us just how confusing guidance may be at the beginning, and how, on following the Angel path, it becomes more and more precise over time. He shares with us his final steps in the world of music, his exile in the USA where, anonymously and in all simplicity, he accompanied one of the richest men in New York State in his terminal phase. He also shares some unrevealed secrets of access that we can have on the collective level, as well as some deep moments of his encounter with different priests and monks, including the Dalaï-Lama.

27. The Concentration of our Intention

On the spiritual level, my perseverance, along with the intensity and concentration of my intention using Angel recitation became my working code to pass through the Gateway of the Stars each night. I used the name of an Angel, and with deeper and deeper, more and more focused, concentrated intention, I asked more and more questions, and hence was able to guide my mind and spirit toward my learning experiences, my apprenticeships. This is when I truly began to feel I was a co-participant in my evolution. I'd choose an Angel, ask my questions, head toward and encounter the answers.

After almost 20 years of initiatic Angel work, I still use this means of functioning today. I now realize that the intensity and concentration of intention was something I had already discovered in the very early days of my spiritual journey. At that time, I taught singing and I had agreed to teach an 11-year-old girl whose heartfelt wish was to be able to sing, but who had great difficulties and sang out of tune on almost every note. I noticed she was very easily distracted and lacked concentration. I asked her to look intently at the piano note I was going to play and to listen to it, then to look at it with all her concentration once again while I played it a second time, and then to sing it. Instantaneously,

she sang the note in tune. I then gave her an exercise to do: to concentrate on a spot on a wall for 5-7 minutes every day. It didn't matter what spot, it could be part of a design on the wallpaper, but she was simply to breathe in and out naturally, and focus on it in silence, closing her eyes for a few seconds when she felt them tire, and then opening them again to continue her focus on the spot on the wall. After a week, her school marks had vastly improved, she was able to sing in tune, and we were able to begin constructing her voice.

28. The Vice President

Concentrating my thoughts on making the right choice was fast becoming a priority for me. I was focusing more and more on my spiritual development, which de-programmed certain aspects and ways of functioning in my life. Just before I gave up music completely, I had begun to record an album in English in New York with the support of Evan Lamberg, then vice president of EMI Publishing. It was the last and most important project I worked on before consciously choosing to end my music career. My agent Ben Kaye, René Angeli's associate, had organized it, and everyone wholeheartedly believed in me. The songs were very spiritual and explained the first stages of my spiritual path and questioning. I worked on this project and had wonderful exchanges and sharing with my producer, Russ DeSalvo, as well as successful songwriters, Arnie Roman, Terry Cox, and all the beautiful people I was working with. But, on the inside, within me, I could feel that the end of this stage was near, even though the doors of the whole world were wide open for me on the music level, even though everything seemed programmed to succeed.

One day, after dreaming *that my white car entered the EMI white limousine,* the phone woke me; it was Evan Lamberg calling. He had just heard the first songs I had co-written and recorded with Russ and Arnie, and the song *Seven Seconds Too Late** had moved him so deeply that he had been speechless as he listened to it in his car. He told me it was one of the most beautiful songs he had ever heard since *Fields of Gold* by Sting, whom he was also working with. I was very moved by his evident sincerity. I could feel that he truly wanted to help and protect me.

In his enthusiasm, he gently began telling me he saw great worldwide success on the horizon, that we would start working on my style of clothing, my hair, my look… My response was a categorical, electric "No, I don't want anyone to tell me how to dress or do my hair! I'm sorry Mr. Lambert, but that's just not me." I asserted myself more intensely that I ever had before. Despite the beautiful dream I'd had announcing phenomenal advancing, I could have offended him, shattered the positive dynamics, lost his confidence, his trust, lost this relationship, but, at the same time, I was proud of having respected myself on this level for the very first time. I, who in the past, had always wanted to please, who had always wanted to make sure I never offended anyone, now, if I had to, I was ready to lose everything in order to follow my angelic ideals. Music was no longer the be all and end all; music in itself was no longer important. Deep down, I knew that if this album came to be, it was only to serve the Angel cause, only to help make Angels known on Earth. Mr. Lamberg immediately replied kindly, "I understand. I work with Barbara Streisand and Sting, and they are like that too. You react like them; they don't want anyone to intervene on this level either. That's okay, we'll respect your choices." And he invited me to attend the Whitney

---

**Song included in Kaya's new album BORN UNDER THE STAR OF CHANGE*

Houston première in New York so we could spend some time together, discuss things, and meet people.

I took a plane to attend the event. The limousine waiting to pick me made me feel ill-at-ease. The vast hotel suite bothered me when I saw the homeless sheltering in doorways, sleeping in the streets. The evening meals in the biggest, top restaurants made me feel dizzy. The première with Whitney and her team, everything anyone could hope for regarding success was right there in front of me, but all of it just whirled and swirled confusedly, echoing emptily in my mind. I was no longer capable of feeling abundance without deep awareness and true conscience. All those people greeting each other, exchanging seemingly delighted, warm *Hellos!* but in reality, not really wanting to get to know each other at all. There was so much hypocrisy. Today, at times like this, at events like these, I am capable of being a good diplomat, a good secret agent, but at that time, extremism was in the process of emerging; the hermit in me was taking shape, and it was stronger than anything else.

29. An End to Music

During that time, the first eight songs of the album were completed and Evan Lamberg organized a showcase evening in New York to present the album to EMI Blue Note and its artistic director. EMI had spent a fortune on this one, unique evening. For this decisive evening, once again I had the best musicians in New York under the direction of my producer, Russ DeSalvo. Everything was mapped out for the album to become a great success, while in my hotel room, I prayed to God, asking Him if He really wanted me to do this, if I was in my rightful place. I felt a constant inner struggle as to whether I should continue in this music world or give it all up.

We received the reply from the prestigious company associated with EMI, Blue Note Records, and it was yes. Evan Lamberg was so happy he phoned me himself to tell me, but I wasn't happy at all. Without saying anything, I tried to understand why God wanted me to continue in this world. The Blue Note contract was due to arrive within the following three weeks. And, sure enough, we duly received it, but we also heard that the artistic director who had taken on the project had been dismissed. Evan told me that we would have to present the album again as well as look around for new record companies since new directors usually arrived with their own projects. Over the next 2-3 months, he presented the project again to several other record companies, and to his great surprise, every single one of them said yes. However, afterwards, all of the company directors who'd said yes were either transferred or dismissed, and so our project fell through. Evan and my agent Ben were dumbfounded. They had never heard nor seen the likes of it. As for me, during that period, I learned that Up Above no longer wanted me to continue in the music business.

After the avalanche of impossible, surprising replies, I received a series of dreams that answered my prayers and questions. In one of these dreams *I saw a guide from the Parallel Worlds, and in the dream, it was as though I had the same potential as Elvis Presley, so great was my potential success. I saw the guide looking intently and directly at me, and each time the phone rang with a positive answer, he simply cut the phone line.* I was so happy to receive that dream confirming what I was feeling in my heart of hearts. From now on – as I thought at the time, before my books became very successful all over the world – my task in life was to be an anonymous angel serving God on Earth. I let things take their course, knowing fine well that Evan wouldn't be able to find a contract no matter how optimistic he was, telling me that this music didn't belong to a particular era, that it was new and inspiring. I waited a certain length of time and then wrote a letter to himself and my agent, thanking them, and informing them that I had decided to turn the page, that for me, music was over.

30. Exile in Cold Springs, New York

I made the decision to go into exile for a while in the United States because at that time, in Quebec, Canada, not a day went by without my being the butt of jokes and mockery on the number one TV show and radio stations. People looked strangely at me, avoided me, were afraid of me, even though I had done nothing other than share my faith and reveal the first steps of my spiritual journey in public interviews. I remember well that I didn't want to do these interviews. I had to receive several dreams before I accepted.

In the first dream I received before my public interviews *I saw the US president's limousine come to fetch me and I had all those bodyguards there to protect me as I went on TV.* I felt really good during my first TV interview in spite of judgmental, critical looks from many people who knew me from childhood. I did some very important interviews over a period of about three weeks before calling a halt and stopping completely. I now understand that I was sowing seeds for the future, that being laughed at and scorned was going to help me surpass criticism, and strengthen and solidify my values, because, while my first book had taken everyone by surprise, startling and astounding almost everyone, years later, my books became top sellers in bookstores, supermarkets, etc., in Quebec (Canada), and in many other countries.

At the height of this period of public mockery, I got a call from Terry Cox, one of the songwriters I'd worked with on the album I'd just done in New York. She told me that a family in Cold Springs was looking for help for a person in his terminal phase. I offered to come and help them, and thus became a volunteer carer and companion for an 84-year-old cancer patient in his terminal phase. He was one of the richest men in New York. He had made his fortune in real estate and was the owner of numerous buildings in New York City. His family wanted to pay me but I refused. I found myself looking after a simple, modest man, and I was very happy God had chosen me to accompany him. In a way, I too was *dying*. I was undergoing deep change, and I knew it was no coincidence that I was there. I knew I was going to learn a lot from him. The family had put a tiny staff apartment at my disposal in their villa in Cold Springs and I was delighted to be there, glad to live anonymously, in great simplicity. I felt better there than in any of the large houses I'd had or lived in previously. I'd asked Terry not to say who I was, hence I was able to live in prayer and divine service, safe from prying eyes.

I looked after this gentleman and I also helped his aging wife. I wore a white uniform all day long and that pleased me well, since the color white symbolizes spirituality. I felt I was serving God, and while looking after this man, I also developed my metaphysical capacities and my angelic conscience by invoking the Angels. Each night my awareness and knowledge grew and expanded. I worked and studied as much at night in my reflections, meditations and dreams, as by day helping these people, and this gave real meaning to my life. I was becoming more and more of an angel in my daily life, thereby fulfilling my dearest wish.

31. Miraculous Healing

This man in his terminal phase had beautiful, natural wisdom. He fully deserved to be well taken care of and the longer I accompanied him, the better I understood why Up Above had sent me to his bedside. If it hadn't been me, God would have sent another good person to accompany him because he really deserved it. Very often, rich people get lost in their needs and their egos; they no longer live in reality, and can even become mean in their protective bubbles, in their fears. Once a black nurse came to his bedside and I saw him open his heart and respect her with true love. For him, there was no difference between races. Although we all know how the older generations sometimes live by old mental measuring sticks, and can easily have all sorts of prejudices, he had absolutely none. I remember congratulating him, telling him few people of his age had as much wisdom and respect for humanity.

I lived at this man's side for several months until he passed away and I received as much from him as he received from me. We didn't talk that much but while looking after him, washing him, feeding him, giving him a drink, and so on, I anticipated his thoughts, his movements. Sometimes we were in perfect symbiosis and he would look at me astonished, not knowing what to say, not understanding who I was. I soon became a great mystery for his family. His visiting children wondered where I'd come from, how I'd been chosen. I maintained the mystery and avoided questions so as not to go into any detail and reveal who I was, or who I had been, because I didn't actually want to be anyone; I just wanted to be a kind, loving, angelic presence. His wife was even a little jealous of my presence. I discreetly left the room whenever I felt her emotions or vibrations. She was a more self-centered, slightly complicated person, while her husband was quite the contrary. He and I even had similar personalities. Near the end of his life, he openly asked me, "Are you an angel?" I whispered yes, and told him that I served God, that He had sent me to help him because of all of his good actions in life. I often visited him in my dreams. I saw his past life, what he had done, and the meaning of my presence at his side. We constantly communicated by telepathy and at one point I saw that he realized, that he knew what we were doing.

In the last weeks of his life, his children and his grandson caught a virus and got sudden diarrhea. Given his great fragility, the family were forbidden to go near him. I'll always remember that time. I felt a sudden fatigue, a great decrease in energy, and I went to lie down to rest and pray. I could feel my tummy gurgling, and I knew that it was very likely that I too had caught that virus. In complete detachment, I nodded off for a few minutes and I received a very powerful dream. *A white-bearded sage all dressed in white emerged from a magnificent Light and said to me, "One day, you will be able to heal yourself." And then he cast a beam of Light on my stomach.* I immediately woke up feeling fine and healthy, inwardly aware that I was to stay and help this man till his last breath; that his passing away was as much a re-birth for me as it was for him.

32. Amazing Grace and A New Mission

I used to sit him up in his chair and sometimes I'd play the piano for him. One of the melodies I composed at his side has become the meditation music that accompanies Angel Iezalel, in the *Angelica Musica* CD collection that I later worked on, which comprises an original melody for each Angel. Angel 13 Iezalel's main quality is fidelity. I played it for him and he asked me what I wanted to do in the future. I told him I was going to found a university, to have a non-profit foundation, and help people learn about work with Angels, dreams and signs. He replied with great serenity and so much love, "I'll be there at the opening of your university." I was deeply moved by these words and said, "You know, of course, that nothing exists yet; so far, I only see it in dreams. There's nothing concrete for the moment, and I don't think there'll be anything before ten years or more." I knew very well that he would have passed away by then, since it was only a matter of days then.

Ten years later, without any knowledge of this story, the first tune my daughter learned to play on the piano was the music of Angel 13 Iezalel. As I listened to her play it as a birthday present for me, tears gently streamed down my cheeks. In my mind's eye, I saw my

84-year-old friend once again telling me, "I'll be there to help you."
I saw all my inner sufferings, all the nightmares, the thousands
of miles I'd had to travel before founding *Universe/City Mikaël
(UCM)*, before my angel foundation could exist, before my books
became known in numerous countries throughout the world. In
the notes my daughter played, I could hear him say, *"I'll be there to
help you,"* and thinking of him, gently weeping, with all my heart
and soul I thanked all those people who helped and supported the
foundation by giving their time and donations, which still support
my Mission *via* Universe/City Mikäel (UCM) today. I understood
that God had spoken to me through that man, that all those people
were the fulfillment of his prediction that he would be there to
help me. Because although I had indeed had phenomenal dreams
explaining the reason for my presence on Earth, explaining my
Mission, I couldn't see it concretely at that time. At that time,
everything I had done for God had de-programmed my life and
led to difficulties and suffering more than anything else. At that
time, I felt I was all alone, with no career, no friends, no family,
and apparently no future.

I had followed all the indications in total trust and obedience.
I had turned the page on a life of glory and fortune that most
people dream of. I considered with detachment all of the marvelous
messages received in dreams announcing the future of my divine
actions, trying not to think about it, not knowing what to do
with this clearly announced, and yet still so unreal, unbelievable
destiny. To remain detached, with no expectations, I sometimes
told myself that beautiful dreams could be mirages, tests to purify
my humility, to render it more divine, and help me become a
better soul.

I now understand what dying to our ordinary conscience means,
and what being reborn to an angelic conscience means. I know that
when we set out on a spiritual journey, when we decide to walk
a spiritual path, in the beginning, we encounter and experience
more negativity than positivity. I know that the purpose of trials
and ordeals is to help us discover our divine nature and a concept
of life and the Universe that is not based on material results, but
rather on qualitative, virtuous results. I believe with all my mind,
heart and soul that, initially, everything, absolutely everything that
we encounter and experience on our path as a spirit in a physical

body serves solely to teach us to become detached from matter so as to develop real, true spiritual connection with God. When we have learned and integrated this, then, and only then, can we live a concrete life where we actually marry spirit and matter, where our first and foremost priority, our one and only goal in life, is to develop Qualities, Virtues and Powers in their purest state. I also know that without Knowledge, without guidance, this can be a turbulent, dangerous journey. However, I believe that future generations will have books like this and many others to help them construct an angelic life from the beginning, instead of having to de-construct and rebuild later, as most of us today have to do, before attaining real, true spiritual objectives.

My friend's death was revealed to me in a dream, and as I very often do today with other souls, I was able to accompany and help him on his way. The night he died, I dreamed *I was with him and he was now deceased. He was lost and didn't know what he was supposed to do. I took him by the hand and said, "It's ok; it's me, Kaya." He recognized me and was clearly relieved. I signaled him to go on toward the tunnel of Light that was ahead of us. He looked at me and went off in that direction.* The following morning, I opened his bedroom door and saw his wife lying crying at his side. He had passed away.

His son was very thankful for all I had done and asked me to come to the funeral, where I ended up singing *Amazing Grace*. Terry, the friend who had introduced me to this family was present, and she introduced me to another family who lived in the region, who had gotten wind of how I'd helped. Knowing I had to leave my present accommodation, they offered me lodgings in exchange for gardening work. The inhabitants of the village of Cold Springs were beginning to wonder who I was, where I came from, because the way I'd taken care of this man in his terminal phase, and the way I'd sung *Amazing Grace* had filled the church and all those present with incomprehensible, powerful, vibrant energy. I willingly accepted this new invitation to serve, knowing in my heart of hearts that another Divine Mission awaited me. The new family was also a lovely family; the lady was spiritual and the couple had just had a beautiful baby girl called Grace.

33. Mystery; Anonymity

Life as a gardener suited me perfectly. I had warned the family that gardening took me time, that I prayed and invoked Angels as I did the work, and I hoped that was ok for them. They very kindly accepted. One lovely Sunday afternoon, we did some weeding all together, and I explained to them that each time I did any weeding, I simultaneously *weeded* my conscience, that's why it took time. Although they weeded at least five times the surface area I did, they respected me and my way of working. Later, Carolyn, the lady who had welcomed me and provided lodgings, told me that the following year, Tim, her husband, was very moved by this teaching because the area I had worked on had remained clear of weeds, whereas lots of weeds had grown back again in all of their sections.

The time I spent with them allowed me to continue to work deeply on myself, to become familiar with my angelic powers on the collective level. I remember Carolyn came into my room one day and saw several newspaper cuttings on major events in the USA and other countries on my bed. There was a great silence and she was clearly a little scared to see all that, not knowing who I was, or where I came from, etc. It was also very intense for me to act and help people, or to see the future in dreams and be able to validate it afterwards with information in the newspapers. This period of my life was very important for me on that level because my inner confidence in these capacities, which we can all develop one day, grew and expanded, and I also explored the different facets and multi-dimensional impacts that we can achieve with our angelic conscience in dreams. Until then, I had intervened a lot on individual levels, and now I realized we can also have an impact on the collective levels. It was fascinating for me. Most of the time when this happens, we see ourselves in a current concrete event in a dream, and we become an integral part of the program. We act as though we knew what to do, but on awakening, we are surprised by what we saw and did in the dream, and we realize that we have come back with confidential information.

At first, when we begin having access to the collective level, we are not strong enough to make decisions ourselves, nor to understand what is going on, what needs to be accomplished, and so we become part of the program, we become one of the symbols that acts concretely but doesn't consciously know what it is we are doing. It's quite an amazing paradox to enter *Intersky* or *Skynet* in the Parallel Worlds, to meet and converse with the president of a country, or see and attend an event that will have major global impact before it occurs, etc., and then read or hear about the consequences of what we saw, experienced or did in the newspapers or on the news. At that period in my life, I even thought about contacting the FBI or the CIA to help them in their searches. For quite a while, I wondered if my mission was to help them, but over time, I understood that it was preferable to remain anonymous since I could always tell the policeman in dreams where to look, to go to such and such a place, and I had learned that *via* his intuition, he could receive the answer and wake up the following day with an idea that would guide him to the solution. I also received in dreams that it was wise for me to always remain anonymous, that an angel had no need to justify himself or prove what he could do.

34. The Reverend Minister and the Dalaï Lama

At the beginning, I sought a cause to serve. I thought the structure of a spiritual community would be good for me. Once I tried to go on retreat with Benedictine monks. I thought the best solution for me might be to retreat into a monastery. I remember what happened and how I felt as clearly as if it took place only yesterday.

The monk who led me upstairs to my room was strange and I felt wary. I felt he was looking at me as a possible victim. Once I'd put my suitcase down in the tiny room, he looked intensely at me and asked if everything was ok, if I had everything I needed. I felt and saw in his eyes that he desired me physically. This was confirmed in his honey sweet tone of voice and manner, which was far from healthy. He was so intense I felt like a prisoner. After I'd said everything was fine, he left me alone. I sat on the bed for 2 or 3 minutes, thinking rapidly, forming a perfectly clear idea: I had to get out of there, leave that place, God had shown me this was not my path, that I was better off meditating and praying in my mountain chalet. I flew downstairs to get away from that place as fast as my legs would carry me.

Another time I became friends with a Baptist minister in Cold Springs. He was a good man and I was able to talk and share quite deeply with him. He helped me by giving me English lessons. He was very lonely and lived in an untidy, disorderly apartment. I lived my life analyzing everything like a dream. With my knowledge of symbolism, I had learned that *everything Above has its likeness here below, and everything here below has its likeness Above.* Spending time with him, I had noticed that he was amazingly kind and very good at helping others, listening to them, inspiring them to discover their faith. He was also very animated when he gave his sermons and preached. Generally speaking, he was a lovely person. But there was a discrepancy between his collective life and his intimate life. In his home, his sadness and solitude were palpable.

We talked for hours. I always kept my spiritual identity veiled, hidden, a mystery, a secret. I had once revealed it to a Catholic priest and he had become afraid of me, of my dreams and nightmares, and stopped returning my calls. After such experiences, where any real sharing on my part always seemed to end up in rejection and fear, I remained silent about my hidden life and angelic powers.

However, I did talk to this minister about work with the 72 Angels, which he found fascinating. He even started invoking the Angels himself. He told me he was really looking forward to my writing a book about Angel work. The day came when I sensed that it was time to end our relationship. As well as the money I owed him for the English conversation lessons, I gave him quite a large sum of money in an envelope so he could renovate his apartment. I was so happy to do this. I knew we were connected beyond this life, and that I was simply returning something he'd already given me.

My trips from Cold Springs to New York City to see another 80-year-old man were also very intense for me. The few times I went downtown, I would deliberately spend 2-3 hours walking to his place rather than taking a bus. I'd sense and feel the thoughts and strong emotions of the passers-by. The intensity of this huge metropolis was so powerful that it electrified me sometimes. My collective conscience was in full expansion and went from one person to another, and like a computer, I'd analyze the different ambiances at top speed. I sensed, felt, analyzed, and validated the numerous soul-states all around me.

The man's name was Ken Appleman, and his wife Ariette was in her 90s, if I remember rightly. I spent whole afternoons talking philosophy with him. Ken helped me a lot by giving me proof of who I was. He too received very precise dreams and he knew about my Angelic Mission on Earth. That did me good because he motivated me, and he sometimes brought me additional keys to information I had received during the night. I cannot say I learned spiritual things with him, because with the more than 50 dreams I received per night, I was very often in advance of everything I experienced and encountered. Nevertheless, I was fascinated that we could talk to each other on this level of conscience. We spent a long time together and I have very fond, deep memories of his paternal presence and affection. After I left New York, I plunged deep into my hermit initiations and no other opportunities arose for us to remain in touch.

I also went to see an Indian guru several times. I was still constantly searching and every night I'd verify in my dreams if these encounters were indications of the path to follow. I was able to check in my dreams if the guru was false or true, and studying the way they functioned also helped me unite the physical and the metaphysical. Understanding that *everything Above has its likeness below* and *vice versa* allows us to validate a lot of information on the spiritual level. When things on the material level are dirty, disorganized, too detached or too materialistic, this outer disheveled, disordered state of things reveals a lot about the inner state. This is true for the director of a company as well as the company itself, for an individual citizen and a whole country, and also for a spiritual current. We should be vigilant on this level, open our eyes, analyze, and evaluate wisely, and hence find good influences and the right people, those we need for the stage of evolution we are going through. I enjoyed the stages where I met with Hindus, Jews, and Muslims, when I observed, sought, and found truths all along the way, while learning to separate the wheat from the chaff.

One day, I thought I should join the Tibetan monks. I was sure that was going to be my path. What's more I felt guided to this path because the Dalaï Lama had appeared in one of my dreams, and in the dream, he'd invited me to come and meet him. When I woke up thinking I had to go to India, I heard that the Dalaï Lama was currently giving teachings in a Buddhist center near Cold Springs, NY. Off I went, heart and soul ready to serve, sure that this was the calling I'd been seeking, sure that this was the place for me, that this was the place where I was supposed to be. Once I got there, I could see that literally thousands of people were there for the event too.

At lunchtime, on my way to the toilet, I took a wrong door and found myself at a large table with all the lamas, the Dalaï Lama's principal advisors. To my greatest astonishment, there was a free place at their table, and quite naturally, they beckoned me to sit down and eat with them. I was both surprised and not surprised at the same time; it was as though it was perfectly normal that I should be there. I spoke to the lama beside me and asked if he ever had dreams. He said that he did but not very often. I told him that it was very intense for me. He immediately shared a dream of his for me to interpret. *He had dreamed that the water was calm and serene and that there was a beautiful mountain.* I easily interpreted that for him, telling him that the day before or after this dream, he had had beautiful stable emotions, and the mountain showed that he'd had a desire for natural elevation on the material level, because the earth element is related to the world of action and matter. He surely had had a wonderful, serene day of meditation and reflection. He was very happy with my interpretation and smilingly indicated that I should go and sit beside an older monk, who seemed to be the most important monk there. "What's your name?" asked the older monk. "Kaya," I replied. "Do you know what that means?" he asked. "No, I don't, but maybe you do? I have always been intrigued as to the meaning of my name. I received it in a dream." He smiled at me and looked at all the other lamas who were listening intently, and very solemnly he said to me, "One of the main goals of Tibetan Buddhism is the *Dharma-Kaya*, which, in Sanskrit, means *embody the dharma, embody spiritual life*." I thanked him and intuitively knew I shouldn't ask any more questions, that I should be very humble. I went back to my place and ate my lunch in silence, listening to the monks, observing them, and living this moment as an exceptional moment in life. I knew in my very cells that I already knew this energy, this way of living, very well.

The night after this experience, I received dozens of dreams and Teachings. The most important one was with the Dalaï Lama himself. *I was with him and he looked at me and said, "You have no business being here; you have a different Mission. You have to leave, otherwise you will end up in Dharamsala doing craftwork!"* Oof! I woke up startled by the power and intensity with which he had delivered his message. The following day, I went back to the Buddhist center to continue listening to the Dalaï Lama's teachings, hoping that he might have seen me in a dream, that he'd recognize me and come and speak to me. I asked the young lama I'd spoken to the previous day if he could get me an audience with the Dalaï Lama. He said he would see what he could do. A few minutes later, the Dalaï Lama's personal secretary came to see me in person. He came right up to where I was sitting and told me the Dalaï Lama would see me. I was truly happy. For me it was a gift from Heaven, and I hoped with all my heart that the Dalaï Lama had seen me in a dream too. After the teaching session was over, I waited patiently in a room where the secretary had asked me to wait. An hour or so later, the secretary came back in, gently apologizing and telling me something last minute had arisen, which meant that I couldn't meet the Dalaï Lama, he had to leave right away. It was the last day of the Dalaï Lama's teaching weekend. I now had an even better understanding of my dream telling me I had to leave and go on toward my own, as yet unknown, destiny.

CHAPTER FOUR
THE TRANSFORMATION

A human-being's transformation toward an angelic conscience is a powerful phenomenon that gradually gives us access to real, divine powers, that we can manifest as much in the concrete world as in the world of dreams. Healing a person's cancer was a landmark in the development of Kaya's new life. Sharing his life experience, he also explains that to integrate an angelic conscience, to become an angel, we have to cleanse our memories, cleanse our distortions that we can study through our dreams and nightmares, as well as through the resonance we have with the people we encounter in our daily lives. He transmits the knowledge that we must de-dramatize our nightmares, our negative experiences, and understand that life is like a dream, that others are parts of us, that we live in a universe of apprenticeship and evolution so as to develop qualities and virtues, and become a better soul. Hence we discover that each physical or metaphysical experience is a source of wisdom and development, gradually leading us to activate our divine capacities.

35. The Power of Healing

Almost 20 years ago, I gave private singing classes at the Vincent D'Indy Music School. One of my singing students, tears in her eyes and brimful with emotion, shared her pain with me as she told me her mother had cancer. My student had very strong faith and she told me she was praying and hoping for her mother's healing with all her heart and soul. She really believed healing was possible. This girl often saw me in her dreams and she deeply trusted me. During lessons, we spoke openly about our spiritual paths. My students and I often spent more time discussing spirituality than singing. I told them that essentially singing was the communication of our soul, our values, our inner world on the positive and negative levels. For me, each song was a responsibility, a creator of atmosphere and ambiance that influenced people and our way of living and materializing. One day this girl looked at me quite spontaneously and said, "I've got a feeling you could help my mother. Would you pray for her, please?" There was so much depth, sincerity and truthfulness in her request, I immediately felt I ought to help her, that it was my duty to try and help.

I've always known that we cannot heal everyone. I often explained to people that illness and physical blockages were essentially teachings for the soul, that they were the result of an accumulation of blockages in our past memories, and their main purpose was to help us develop qualities. I knew and also said that miracles were possible, and that we all had the power to heal or treat ourselves, and even heal others. Thinking like this was perfectly natural for me; it was concrete and real, and I was convinced we all had such powers. My relationship with the power of healing had always been mysterious, veiled, and sacred. I knew in my heart that I was capable of it, but I had never actually dared to try. I was afraid of deluding others, so I preferred not to tell anyone what I was capable of.

However, this student's deep request, and the current of energy pervading me when she asked, felt like a calling, a sign signaling that I had the authorization to heal her mother, so I made the decision to try and use my healing powers for someone I didn't know, for the first time. Simultaneously I felt uncertain, divided between doing it or not doing it, because I wanted to be sure I wasn't interfering with God's plans, with this person's life plan. I was also naturally convinced that healing was in God's hands. Deep down, I had the innate knowledge that if we don't succeed in healing a person, it's because the Divine Program doesn't allow it. When we do succeed, it's because healing was part of the Divine Plan, and not thanks to any personal super powers.

There is always a reason for everything that happens, for what we go through in our life, and sometimes illness is a gift of evolution that is necessary for our soul. Today, with my wife, Christiane, and Dr. François Bouchard and his wife Denise Fredette, we have founded the *Angelica Pratica Clinic*, a clinic for energy healing in Canada. For years now I have taught numerous doctors, nurses, and therapists about the relationship that exists between illness, the patient, and the capacity to heal people or relieve their suffering. Several books on the capacity to heal physically and metaphysically using symbolic language and work with the Angels are presently being written, and will be published and distributed worldwide by our foundation in the next few years.

Very often doctors or healers feel ill at ease in situations where the treatment of certain patients gives no results. I always explain to them that sometimes we can help, treat, heal, or guide a person toward medication and/or medical procedures that will give him a second chance, but total healing is only possible when the underlying memories have been completely cleansed and transformed. That is why so many healings remain partially, superficially successful, and not deeply so. That is why we can treat certain illnesses either traditionally or energetically but they still don't heal. Illness is an accumulation of negative memories. It can be decoded using symbolic language, which helps us get to the heart of certain behavior and experiences, discover their true nature, and what kinds of emotional, intellectual and/or spiritual dynamics have been accumulated, sometimes over a very, very long period of time, even beyond this life. Our soul is a true living computer that continually records sequences of information right down into our DNA, thereby creating our body and realities that reflect who we are in the depth of our memories. Our body is formed in accordance with the soul-states, qualities and weaknesses we have within ourselves. It is so important to understand the metaphysical aspect of illness on the symbolic level as well as in terms of memories, and not only on the horizontal, physical level.

This first healing experience was carried out in secret. After my student's request, I began to focus my mind and spirit on her mother and every day I prayed for her, saying the *Our Father* over and over again like a mantra. On my knees, in meditation, several times a day I prayed to God, asking Him that if it was right for this woman's soul, then for her to be healed. Although I'd only seen this woman once or twice, I saw myself fuse with her and I breathed in the Name of God through her so she could heal. At the same time, although I knew healing was possible, that I could do it, I felt perplexed because I had never actually used my healing powers. After what I'd done for Kasara's mother, this experience was also a test for me to see if I truly was capable of healing.

The following week, my student called to tell me her mother was better. The doctors didn't understand what had happened, but she herself was convinced that I had prayed and healed her. I didn't say yes or no but, deeply moved by my silence, in a voice trembling with emotion, she thanked me, knowing in her heart that I had intervened. When I put down the phone, I was very happy and simultaneously afraid that people would hear of this. The fear of revealing my spiritual identity and capacities was still so present in me. It took intense work on myself to surpass this fear, because, for me, revealing spiritual powers meant suffering. I had to spend a long, long time working on the memories that dwelt in me, inscribed and recorded therein in a distant past, and revived by the media rejection and mockery I'd experienced in my recent past.

A few months later a friend of mine called me in a terrible state; he'd just been diagnosed with brain cancer. I was in the car on my way to his place when he called. He had kindly offered to put me up immediately after my separation from Kasara's mother. He'd given me a room in the basement until I had time to find a place of my own and re-organize my life. My friend had to leave his job because his cancer was already advanced and he needed to undergo immediate, intense chemotherapy. He and his wife had just had a child, and I could see him worsen each day. I could hear him vomit after the chemotherapy treatments and the news was not good. He was suffering from such a terrible headache that he didn't dare take his child in his arms for fear of dropping him because of the headache and dizziness caused by the pain and his medication. I had to rapidly find somewhere else to live to leave them their intimacy as this ordeal had created great upheaval in their lives. Deep down, I knew I could help my friend, but simultaneously, I didn't completely believe in my capacities; I wasn't 100% confident. Finally, though, I decided to offer my help and give him a treatment, telling him that if I managed to heal him, he had to use his second chance to find a way to serve God on Earth. Ready to do anything to heal, he accepted.

He came to the chalet where I now lived, and lay down on the bed. I explained to him that only God could decide to heal him, but that I would pray and ask for help on his behalf. I didn't really know how to what to do as it was my first time to give someone a physical, concrete treatment. I put on some inspiring background music, lit a few candles, took his head between my two hands and began to pray the *Our Father*. At that time, I didn't know about work with Angel Energies. I began to circulate energy through my hands holding his head, and I added an intention to my prayers, "Dear God, if needs be, take my life in exchange. I am ready to die if I have to so he can heal. May Your Will be done." I continued to say this while repeating the *Our Father* for about 2 hours, and at one point, I felt electricity flow out of my hands and into his head. It was so powerful, I cried out, "Arghhhh!" It was so intense and surprising and lasted about a minute. Then I sat down on the bed, exhausted. A friend of mine who had been there during the treatment, was speechless, while the man who had just received this charge of energy woke up from a deep sleep, not knowing what had happened or where he was. He regained full consciousness after a few minutes. Meanwhile I myself had an incredibly powerful, intense headache exactly where the tumor was situated, whereas his headache was gone. He radiated well-being, while I was suffering so much, I could hardly walk. I reassured him I was fine and asked him where exactly his tumor was located; without telling him I realized that I now had it. My two friends left and I lay down on the bed in prayer and total symbiosis with God. I was fascinated by what I had just experienced, and I went over every detail, every second of what I had felt and experienced during the treatment. My head still ached intensely but I had absolutely no regret that I had said I was ready to give my life in exchange for his. I was ready to die if I had to because in my mind, heart and soul I was convinced that to truly treat and heal, we had to fuse completely, with no fear whatsoever for ourselves. I used this mystical experience to fuse totally with divine trust and I continued repeating the *Our Father* like a mantra. I had a terrible headache but I wasn't in the least afraid for myself. I continued to pray intensely, submitting to God's Will, and it took a long time to fall asleep.

During the night, I received a revealing dream explaining what I had just experienced. In my dream, *I was with my sick friend and the other friend who had been present during the treatment. The three of us were sitting at a table. In the middle of the table there was a bowl full of a black liquid, and I knew that liquid was actually a very dangerous poison. I took a white, absorbent handkerchief and placed it in the bowl to absorb all of the black poison, every last drop. I then went to my friend's toilet and threw the handkerchief full of black poison into the toilet and tried to flush it away. The toilet, however, was blocked, and I had to quickly put my hand into it to extract objects that were blocking the evacuation pipe. One after the other, I took out all sorts of things, including a toy dinosaur and his wedding ring. While I was doing this, he stood beside me and looked sadly at his wife in the distance, because their marriage had been in serious danger for quite some time. I managed to get the toilet to work and I knew that evacuating the dangerous poison, which represented death, would be a difficult operation. After this, I realized that my two-year-old daughter Kasara, wearing a red dress, was in the bath, and her 3rd eye had been contaminated by the poison. "Oh no! no! Kasara!" I said and quickly picked her up in my arms, placed her forehead under the bath tap and I cleansed her 3rd eye with my fingers.* Then I woke up.

The headache remained for 48 hours and I stayed in bed all that time. My friend called me every day to thank me, telling me he no longer had any headache, that it was a real miracle. A few days after this treatment, he saw his doctor and his tumor had completely disappeared without a trace. The doctors were astounded. I'd asked my friend to keep all this a secret, and he did.

Very quickly, my friend found work again, and in a matter of months, he became rich through a very special set of circumstances and synchronicity. Success came easily to him. He opened one restaurant, then another, offering poor quality fast food. I saw him prosper rapidly but there was no sign at all of his promise to serve God, to help humanity. At the same time, he distanced himself from me even though I never reminded him of his promise. Not long after his healing, I'd even sold him my car at a very low price, but he didn't respect his monthly payments and it took him over two years to pay me back. I received a great Teaching as to why God blocks us sometimes, why we may have ordeals in our life. Fifteen years later, without either of us being in touch, while I was writing this book, I had a quick look at his Facebook profile. In his last message in 2011, he boasted about the great score he'd made on a Las Vegas style gambling machine. I now know that Up Above let me have this experience so that I would learn to use my spiritual power and wealth well, and come to an even deeper understanding of the fact that evil is educational, and has its place in the overall divine scheme of things.

36. Kasara's Question

It was difficult to see my daughter immediately following my separation with her mother. This was the greatest ordeal of my life. On account of my spiritual changes, Kasara's mother, who lived and worked in the same artistic environment as me, didn't have it easy. Everyone mocked and scorned me and advised her to stay away from me, not to let me have any custody rights. Given the circumstances, she could easily have done this. If there is one thing that made me cry my heart out, it was that. My new spiritual image and label meant that I was misunderstood and rejected by many people. However, Kasara's mother was very brave as we never had recourse to lawyers. I prayed and prayed and prayed and was ready to accept whatever God decided, and she finally opened her heart, ignored what her entourage thought, and agreed to trust me. She placed no restrictions at all regarding custody. We simply organized it harmoniously between ourselves. We agreed that when our daughter was with her, she would adapt to her mother's world, and when she was with me, to mine. Hence we respected each other and everything worked out fine. A few years later when I began to lecture in different countries, Kasara did school by correspondence because her mother also travelled all over the world. Thus, with Christiane and me, Kasara learned in an environment of spiritual abundance, and with her mother, in one of great material abundance.

Kasara was naturally a very gifted child on the psychic and spiritual level. It was, and is, absolutely fascinating to have the experiences we had together, and continue to have today. Kasara is now 20 years old, which is the age of my intense spiritual path. As soon as she arrived on Earth in 1993, my life was totally transformed. She was only 2 or 3 years old when sometimes I'd wake up in tears after my intense nightmares, and she would come over to me, caress my hair, and I'd hear her little voice say, "It's ok, Daddy; it's going to be ok." She had such natural inner strength. She could have been frightened to see her father cry, but, on the contrary, she knew, her soul knew, what I was going through, that it was good for me, for my evolution, for what I would become over time. As she looked gently, lovingly and confidently at me, she was so beautiful, luminous and pure that it made me cry even more!

She also answered all of my thoughts and emotions, even before she could talk. We were so connected that I would be thinking about something, a dream or a problem, or whatever, and she'd come up to me holding out a toy, which was a symbol that gave me an answer. In fact, as she kept doing this, it was with her that I actually learned to apply symbolic language. Then, when she began to talk, she used to say apparently incoherent things, but I always listened to her with symbolic language, and understood that she was already teaching me, advising me about my decisions, so much so that when I didn't know what to do, I asked Up Above to talk to me through Kasara. I'd wait till she started up a conversation with me and I'd listen attentively in symbols to what she said, and that was how I'd receive my answer. I learned to do this with her, and I still often do so today when I'm with other people or children. I listen and the other person teaches me, telling me whether he is ready or not to receive help or to speak about a certain subject, or simply telling me how he is, what he is experiencing deep within. Symbolic language is powerful because everyone speaks on multi-levels, without being aware of it. Hence, conversations about the weather are always interesting!

Once when Kasara was about 3½ years old, she said to me, "Life is eternal but can we become an animal… can we incarnate as an animal?" I replied rather vaguely, not really very sure of the answer myself. That night she came to visit me in a dream to rectify what I'd said. In the dream *I saw her as the child she was, the same age as she was in concrete reality, and all of a sudden, she began to grow and grow and grow and she became a guide, an Asiatic type of man, who told me in a powerful, very precise voice, "Animals and humans are two different things!"* Reincorporating my physical body and all of my physical senses, I woke up stunned to have seen my daughter like this. I didn't sleep for the rest of the night I was in such a hurry to transmit this Teaching to her that she herself had just taught me! I remember going into her room and sitting by her bed, caressing her hair, tears of deep, deep love for her streaming down my face. When she woke up the next morning, she came into my room as usual and found me in meditation. I brought up the question she'd asked me the previous evening without mentioning the dream I'd received. I was able to explain to her that human beings and animals were two different things, with complementary programs. I only told her about the Teaching she had transmitted to me after it had been confirmed by several other dreams in the days following the revelation that her *guide-soul* had taught me.

I've always known deep down that we should never boost our child's ego by repeatedly telling him he's wonderful, that love and wisdom are naturally transmitted through experience, and that we need to be careful regarding spiritual ego too. I advise parents to bring up their child normally, not to turn him into a circus act with special powers and hence try to impress family and friends. When we want something too much, less of it or lacks are just around the corner! That's how life works.

37. Continual Adjustments

I spent years adjusting to and integrating the updated data and information that I received, which gradually led to profound transformation. I was so shaken up by my 10-50 dreams per night that helped me evolve, that each day was like a re-birth, giving birth, not to a new self, but to a re-discovered self. When Kasara wasn't with me, Up Above took advantage of my being alone to serve me with violent nightmares and intense *explosions* on both my inner and outer levels. Everything was so well orchestrated that I knew that any weekend Kasara was with her mother would be put to good use by Up Above to help me evolve. Much later, when I watched the TV-film *Taken* by Steven Spielberg, which is about a man who is constantly kidnapped by extraterrestrials, that keep changing place, time, and space…oof! it really spoke to me since that is what I had been going through in my inner world.

From synchronicity to synchronicity, from dream to nightmare, I was evolving, learning to live angelically, to integrate all these experiences in my conscience. I was in a state of perpetual observation of everything that was going on, and my senses now responded differently than they had before I began to invoke Angels. I could sense my mutation, my changes. It was as though I was shedding layer after layer of skin as, one after the other each veil, each illusion, was removed.

I remember walking in the countryside one day. I had meditated so intensely day and night, that out on a concrete walk, when I looked up at a branch of a tree, I actually entered that branch. I penetrated the very heart of the tree's energy and I could feel that state of conscience in my whole body. I was in another dimension and I couldn't see the physical place where I was anymore. It was so powerful, so immense, so calm, so receptive, and so totally alive and vivifying. Life was revealing itself to me in this way so that I could discover it, so that I could sense, feel and integrate the fusion we can have with nature and the whole environment.

When we hurt a tree, when we don't respect the environment, we ourselves are affected. We hurt ourselves because the entire Universe forms a whole, and we are all part of that whole. That's why dreaming of a flower means we we are actually in touch with a feeling, with the living expression of our most marvelous, our sweetest, most gentle, most inspiring feelings and sentiments. The same goes for everyone and everything that exists; they all represent states of conscience, condensed information that has to be organized, structured, and fused with divine qualities so as to become peace and harmony.

Many people seek and desire peace and the unification of all of the different populations on Earth. But this can never be fully achieved as long as we haven't understood that we must first achieve peace and harmony within ourselves. The world we live in is only the tip of the iceberg of what we are on the inside. There is as much violence and negativity within us existing side by side with our positive aspects. Hence the importance of integrating and making Divine Qualities the goal of our life and evolution. Angelic living, becoming angelic, becoming an angel is everyone's goal; consciously or unconsciously, each of us seeks to achieve this goal. The Universe is so good to us it lets us experiment as we do. Our Earth is first and foremost a School where we learn by our mistakes, which leads us to find solutions, create laws and social functioning that also evolve with time and experience.

38. Divine Laws

The Divine Angelic Laws greatly helped me focus and concentrate my conscience on good, especially when I didn't understand the meaning of my dreams, the meaning of my life or other people's lives. Each time I felt ill at ease, or thought there was injustice, or whenever I saw something that I didn't understand, I'd repeat the Law or Laws that related to what I was feeling or going through.

To develop angelic conscience, I kept referring back to the great Principles that I had gradually received in my dreams. There are many Laws, of course, – many more than those listed below – but this summary will help you understand how I was able to re-program the foundations of my life during the most intense, crucial moments of my angelic development.

The Divine Laws of Consciousness are the great Principles that govern the functioning of the Universe; they are the basis of all Creation. Consequently, they also rule over and govern the working of our conscience, justifying and motivating the many pathways of experimentations taken by human beings. When a person knows these Laws, when he recognizes and applies them in his daily life, and uses them to evolve, he becomes receptive to his Creator, to his spiritual nature, and he then applies them consciously. Thereafter, all the mysteries of the Universe can be revealed to him. These Laws are numerous, but to anyone consciously committed to a spiritual path, it is particularly helpful to know, understand and integrate the following 15.

1) GOD IS A LIVING COMPUTER

God is an immense Living Computer that orchestrates the events of the Universe. This Computer manages the life of all beings, including their decisions and acts, and their thoughts, feelings and deeds are recorded, just as computer data is recorded on its hard drive. Based on the principle of free choice, this Living Computer allows each person to experiment, while managing the global Universe for the good of all. In this great Cosmic Computer, each human being has his very own program, in which the parameters of experimentation are established by the spiritual Guides, the various levels of experimentations are pre-programmed and activated at given moments. As Einstein said, "God was certainly not playing dice when he created the Universe."

2) DIVINE JUSTICE IS ABSOLUTE

In the Universe everything is right, in the sense that all events occur in accordance with calculations of infinite precision. When certain situations or ordeals that we go through seem unjust, it's because we carry within us memories of erroneous thoughts, emotions and actions, and reap what we have sown. Humans being are not perfect and during their many incarnations they commit *misactions*[1].

Since the spirit is eternal and consciousness keeps evolving, these misactions must be repaired, and their rectification often requires many lives. As for the evolution of the soul, what happens to us is always right. Therefore, injustice only seems to exist when we consider things from a *horizontal*, non-spiritual point of view; when considered from a *vertical*, spiritual, soul-evolution point of view, there actually isn't any injustice. The soul exists only to improve and become more Divine. When, consciously or unconsciously, we fail in this mission, we reap a karma that, one day or another, we will have to settle. When we understand this Law, whenever we find ourselves in situations where we have a feeling of injustice, it is easier to refer back to ourselves, to go within and purify what needs to be cleansed and purified within ourselves. We can see and understand that what others do is their soul's chosen path to ensure that they evolve, and we remain compassionate toward them.

3) THE LAW OF MULTI-LEVELS

Everything Above has its likeness on Earth, and everything on Earth has its likeness Above.

We live simultaneously on many levels: the physical, emotional, and intellectual levels are but a few of the denser ones. All levels are similar, not in their workings, but in their structure and in their Laws. Observation of the concrete world allows us to understand the other worlds. An initiate knows that what he experiences in his outer world perfectly reflects what he is experiencing within himself. It is for this reason that the study of symbolic language is important.

4) THE LAW OF REINCARNATION

We die and are reborn for the sole purpose of becoming better souls. Our lives serve solely as a place of apprenticeship, grounds

---

1. Misaction ('acte manqué' in French) encompasses the idea of a slip-up, a mishap, a mistake, a blunder, an oversight, forgetting to do what we'd intended to do, a lapsus, an act of omission, any act or non-action that is not right, is not divinely harmonious.

for experimentation. When a person attains sufficiently elevated levels of conscience, limitations that are inherent to physical life disappear. Thereafter such a person no longer needs to reincarnate to live out and settle his karmas. This person develops great metaphysical powers, which allow him to create a universe of lives, of dreams, whose sole aim and purpose is to participate in the evolution of humanity, and help others evolve and become better people, better souls. One day, we profoundly understand that the only reason for our existence is to qualities, virtues, and divine powers.

5) THE LAW OF SYNCHRONICITY

Synchronicity is the universal Principle upon which all situations, both positive and negative, are perfectly planned by the great Living Computer that is God. This is why there is no such thing as coincidence. In order to recognize synchronicity at all times, in all circumstances, we must first have profoundly purified ourselves. To live in this state of grace, which manifests itself even in matter, we must have no more expectations, doubts, or fears. We call this state *angelic dharma*, the embodiment of spiritual life.

6) THE LAW OF RESONANCE

We attract what we are and we resonate with what we are. This Law finds its most concrete equivalence in the mechanical resonance, which states that "All objects have their own natural vibration frequency; oscillation at the same frequency as the natural frequency of an object can make it vibrate." In much the same way, an individual can vibrate or resonate with another individual, with what that individual is, even with his deepest unconscious memories. He can vibrate or resonate positively or negatively. Therefore, the Law of Resonance as applied to human beings – i.e. when we feel attracted to or disturbed by another person – indicates that we are connected to similar memories; we vibrate and resonate with the same wavelength. The Law of Resonance is the Law initiates use most. They apply it daily, because it leads to the highest levels of conscience and deep Knowledge both of ourselves and others, of our individual life and Life in general.

7) THE LAW OF KARMA

We always reap what we sow. If, in our life's garden, we sow Angelic seeds, which are Qualities, Virtues and Powers in their purest state, and if we respect Divine Laws, then the result will be abundance, and we will reap the stability of great spiritual happiness. If we happen to sow poor quality seeds, whether through our thoughts, emotions, behavior or actions, then we reap poverty, ill-being and suffering on many levels.

8) EVIL IS EDUCATIONAL

Evil is a path that leads to good. It is the path Cosmic Intelligence sometimes chooses to make us conscious that a negative action, or a misaction, necessarily engenders a new cycle of evolution. From this perspective, ordeals and suffering are learning situations for the soul. Because, as we have just seen for the Law of Resonance, the negative side of things exists only to help us develop the positive side more deeply; hence negativity is educational.

9) EVIL IS NOT DRAMATIC

From the point of view of our soul's evolution, suffering and pain hardly matter. They represent learning tools and are not at all harmful for our soul. The negative aspect of things, situations, and/or events exists to incite us to develop the positive aspects more deeply. Therefore, evil, wrong-doing, what hurts, is not dreadful or dramatic. In fact, whenever we dramatize evil, we cut ourselves off from the good that dwells in us, we lose sight of the true reason for our experiences and experimentations. Whenever we dramatize evil in any way, we actually amplify negative aspects. The day we find ourselves in the middle of difficult situations and soul-states and we manage not to dramatize, then we will have overcome a great hurdle, made a wonderful breakthrough, and opened ourselves to new perceptions. Ordeals, pain, suffering, and anguish exist for the sole purpose of educating the soul.

10) MATTER IS TEMPORAL AND EDUCATIONAL

Matter in reality is just a form, a pretext, or cover taken by the Spirit for the duration of a life cycle on earth, in order to provide the soul with an opportunity to learn. In this sense, matter is temporal. Consequently, if we consider the material world as having real value in a final, finite sense, if we consider that it is an end in itself, then we are deluded, and live in illusion. Matter serves to help us develop Divine Qualities and Virtues; hence the true reason for its existence is to educate us, to help us learn, evolve and become better people, better souls.

11) ILLUSIONS ARE EDUCATIONAL

Successive events in a person's life correspond to his program, to what he is, and what he must experience. These situations are illusions, which evolve depending on the person's capacity to integrate new concepts. A person living in an ordinary conscience may perceive a situation he is experimenting as positive, but in the eyes of a person who has integrated Knowledge, its appears as a negative experiment. This is because the ordinarily conscious person is not aware of the profound significance and deep meaning of what he's going through: he's evolving in illusion. This illusionary reality exists for educational purposes. We experiment distortions until the day we develop discernment, which allows us to distinguish between good and evil. Everyone does this at his own rhythm. When an initiate understands this Law, he respects the reality of other people's illusions; he respects their rhythm of apprenticeship.

12) DREAMS ARE REALITY

A dream is a means to allow us to better understand the realities of people and things. A dream unveils the profound sense of our actions and the resonances that we experience. It never deceives us, because, it is not deformed by ordinary consciousness. When we understand our dreams, we know where we stand in our evolution. In this sense, it constitutes an evolutive keystone we can trust. For the initiate, dreams eventually become as real as material reality. They become a concrete experience and a doorway opening onto and giving us access to other worlds. One day, we understand that the physical and the metaphysical are one; that life is multidimensional.

13) EVERYTHING IS A STATE OF CONSCIENCE

Human beings pass constantly from one state of conscience to another, even while sleeping. At all times, our state of conscience is either pure and luminous, completely negative, or a distorted, confused mixture of purity and negativity.

14) EVERYTHING IS SYMBOLIC

The physical and metaphysical Universe is mathematical in its original conception. Everything that is encountered in the physical dimension has meaning and significance that originate in the metaphysical dimension. This is true, both in our inner selves as well as our outer selves, in the microcosm as well as in the macrocosm. Everything is symbolic.

15) OUR SPIRIT IS ETERNAL

For Cosmic Intelligence, time is simply a pedagogical tool. It serves as a framework for learning. Since our spirit's sole purpose is to evolve and as its expansion is infinite, the human spirit, i.e. the Divine Spark that dwells in us, is also eternal.

39. To Become an Angel, We have to Cleanse our Needs

I think the most important aspect of the mutation of our ordinary, human conscience toward an angelic conscience is the work we do on the transcendence of our needs. The Divine Laws and Angel Recitation, or Angel Mantra, really help us transcend our multiple needs. Transcendence doesn't mean we eradicate all needs and no longer feel any at all. No, transcendence of our needs means that we now experience and activate needs in symbiosis with our own well-being as well as that of others.

Most people act unconsciously in an ordinary, non-spiritual, or instinctual, animal-like conscience, where the law of the jungle prevails in the choices and actions they take. Why should being hungry or not having had our morning cup of coffee or tea make us impolite, bad-tempered, or even aggressive? Why buy shares in a company that does not respect the environment or ethical laws, whose many poorly paid workers live and work in inhumane conditions in certain countries? Why do we encourage such activities, why do we invest our vital energy, our money, in leisure or other activities and products that have huge collateral effects?

Individual needs are often dismissed as unimportant, having little or no effect in the *grand scheme of things*, but that is only because we evaluate that need in the singular; i.e. without knowing or deeply understanding that if we make a negative gesture, if we take one negative action, and other people make the same gesture, the same decision, then we participate in creating and nourishing systems that are not fair or just, that do not respect equality and equal rights for everyone. Business, commerce, trade is at the

core of people's needs and there is very little conscience in these fields. Each and every one of us who hasn't got a humanitarian conscience and a sense of fairness contributes toward systems that engender gigantic inequalities with seriously harmful, prejudicial collateral effects for millions of people on Earth.

Over the centuries, rich countries have maintained this spirit, this colonialist type of thinking where a short-term, invasive mindset selfishly takes instead of sharing resources fairly, and thinking of the long-term effect of actions and decisions. Living with an angelic conscience means having global vision, not just seeing what we have on our plates, but *seeing* where things, where our food comes from; *seeing* the whole path from the idea, the initial concept to materialization.

Whenever we go to a McDonald restaurant, no matter what part of the world we are in, the minute we enter the restaurant, we are in *McDonald country,* in that particular, easily recognizable egregore[1]. It is fascinating to study collective egregores, the thought-forms of a company, that we can actually feel in concrete reality. Each restaurant in this chain, to give only one example, is governed by the same rules, regulations and ways of working, uses similar products, employs similar management and administrative approaches to set up and organize the restaurant. That is why we feel the same energy from one McDonald restaurant to another, whether it be in Chicago or Tokyo.

Of course, it is true that more and more multi-national companies are slowly beginning to have more respect for human values and fair trade, but a lot of education still remains to be done in this field on our planet. Angelic living means conceiving the spirit, the idea of materialization with right, fair, harmonious conscience. Of course, we shouldn't be utopian; we have to work with the most logical, workable decisions possible. However, we should always be ready to change when the time comes, when it is possible to improve and better things from a spiritual, quality point of view.

When I lecture abroad, I travel by plane, which uses fossil fuel. For the moment, I have no other choice because our human world hasn't yet replaced these polluting forms of energy, hasn't yet found a way of renewing or de-polluting these energies. I can take a plane knowingly, without feeling put out, or disrespectful of Divine Principles, because I know there aren't any solutions for this yet. However, I can assure you that as soon as a better means of planetary transport is found, I shall take it and hence evolve toward what is better. We all behave like this, sometimes following current fashion and social trends, choosing to buy better products, etc., but very often, we seek prices that only correspond

---

1. *An egregore is a reservoir of collective memory, a collective mindset, collective group-thought; it is the vibration that results from the thoughts, emotions, desires, ideals, intentions, and behavior of a group of people, everything in all of the past and present lives of a country, population, or group of people that produces a particular mentality, atmosphere, character, and/or feeling we associate with them. Usually as soon as we cross the border into a different country, we become aware of its different egregore, but a team, a choir, a school, etc., also have their own egregore.*

to quantity, thereby encouraging low range, poor quality products, thereby helping the bottom end of the market to remain active and prosperous. The more a person develops his angelic nature, the more his choices improve until eventually, just by looking at a product, he can use his clairvoyance and clairsentience to perceive essences and decode whether a product is right and fair.

At the beginning of my spiritual path, I remember going into a store one day to buy a pair of trousers. I studied those trousers from all angles. They seemed right but something held me back, so, in the end, I decided not to buy them that day. During the night, I had a dream wherein *I found myself in a developing country, in the factory that made those trousers, and I could see that the factory didn't treat its workers right.* When I woke up, it was clear to me why I had hesitated to buy them.

Now I do that all the time. In my dreams, I find myself in the offices or workplaces of people I'm due to meet, or will meet at some point, long before I actually meet them in the flesh. Hence I know if we have strong enough affinities to form an alliance, go into partnership, work together, etc. We mustn't seek perfection in order to come to a decision because nothing is totally perfect. Our criteria should be the best spiritual and material choice possible at the particular moment in time, according to what has to be done. Otherwise, if we are too purist, we can no longer manifest and we become marginalized. We mustn't forget that our interaction with others sets in motion life changes for them too. All encounters always leave an effect on people. No encounter is ever without a qualitative, evolutive exchange.

Very often, the more spiritual people open their conscience, the less capable they are of materializing and manifesting with others, and they experience great discrepancies. Knowing we are in the right place at the right time is very important, even if we have to change later on for something better, or when the person or situation doesn't evolve in the right direction. An angel is not afraid of fusing with everything that exists. He only seeks to ensure that his presence always leads to change, to evolution toward the Light, while knowing that sometimes his presence may also trigger ordeals for others so that they may cleanse the distortions of their conscience in order to grow, evolve and expand.

90

Very often now I arrive in places where people have been through difficulties before I meet them, which means their energies are more open and more connected to what I represent on Earth. After their difficulties, they are readier to receive help from Above. Angelic Energy is first and foremost an educational force of evolution and integration of Qualities and Divine Powers. Matter only exists to provide grounds for experimentation for our evolution. It is important to always remind ourselves of this especially when something hasn't worked out, hasn't led to the expected results. The path to evolution sometimes takes numerous detours before reaching its goal.

I very often see this in dreams. I'm told to do something because something magnificent will result. I do it and the results are quite ordinary, even mediocre, materially speaking. Later, however, the action and energy that was set in motion fulfills the promise of magnificence and engenders what was shown in my dream. Unless, of course, the dream solely concerned parts of myself, and then the wonderful magnificence that was foretold is experienced on various levels of my inner self, of my conscience. It is very important to define the dream well. Is it only a part of me, or is it a premonitory dream related to materialization and/or other people? When in doubt, we refer back to ourselves, we work on the + and − aspects of the dream in terms of qualities and virtues, and if it is premonitory, we will know and see it take root and flourish later. With time, the more we work on ourselves, the more our unconscious is freed from blockages and negative memories, the easier it is to know whether we are only visiting ourselves or whether we are visiting a precise situation.

CHAPTER FIVE

EXPERIMENTATION

The more we evolve on the angelic level, the more powerful our experimentations become. In this chapter, we see Kaya exploring and developing his divine powers: on the individual level through the angelic help he gives Mike when he could have committed serious violent acts; and through his social involvement on the metaphysical level during the O.J Simpson trial, when the former footballer was first acquitted for the murder of his wife, and later found guilty by a civil court after his deceased wife's family appealed. We also see him act in dreams, attend a birth, receive information before giving a seminar, and other dream experiences. He gradually discovers the important responsibility of his new angelic powers.

40. Saving Mike

I've been providing angelic help for over 18 years now. One of the first people I accompanied was a young man in his twenties. He was a real genius in some fields, but he also had immense, very dangerous, destructive forces in him. His parents had asked me to help him, and they had suggested that he take some time to talk to me. He was really and truly afraid of himself, afraid of what he might do. At that time, he was into drugs, and he felt such incredible destructive energy that he openly threatened to commit suicide. He was like a young man from a good family who could suddenly go into a school and kill dozens of people. He was full of prejudices and simultaneously had a perfectionist, over categorical, even extremist side. When contradicted, a combative, vengeful force would be activated in him and become almost uncontrollable. His personality was very much focused on his ego, his personal needs, and on seizing power. He always wanted to be right and to have the last word.

His parents, who worked with the Angels, were among my and my wife's first students, and became the first voluntary workers for the association, had asked me to help their son. I told them that the request for help had to come from him and not them. It took their son all his courage to call me. Not only was he not interested in Angels, but confiding in others wasn't his strong point either. He was the kind of person who thought he was *a real man,* but who was actually too masculine, too macho and easily vexed, all of which I perceived in the very first words of his phone call. He was also stiff and rather sharp while making his request as though doing his best to make me refuse. People who don't feel good about themselves, and are not well on the inside, are more often than not their own worst enemy, because they limit themselves. They sometimes have an attitude of repulsion deeply embedded in their personality. Not loving themselves, they seek to hurt others, to project their suffering on the outside like emotionally awkward, rebellious teenagers who say the opposite of what they'd actually like to say.

I accepted his request with all my heart and suggested we go for a walk together. He confided in me that he was at the end of his resources, that he was afraid of himself and what he might do. He said, "Things just keep spinning in my head! I'm full of such negative, aggressive, destructive thoughts that I'm afraid of what will happen, what they'll make me do. They are so terrible, I'm

94

afraid of them myself. Can you help me?" I replied, "The only person who can help you is God. It's your spiritual path that can make all the difference, because the evil is not in your body – he was actually a top-level athlete – it's in your mind."

He also told me that he loved his parents but when he was angry, he became so violent he couldn't control himself. I knew he took drugs but I could tell he wasn't ready to stop because he minimized, he trivialized his consumption. For him, taking drugs calmed him down, relieved his tension, and helped him forget, *escape*, because he didn't like his life. He talked to me about this theoretically, as though it were all right from him to take drugs, that society didn't understand people who took drugs. He didn't make the link between a petty thief and a bank robber. Major theft always begins with a person stealing just a small packet of sweets. The person minimizes and accepts his behavior, dabbles in petty theft for a while before gradually getting involved in more serious theft, until the day he is capable of robbing a bank.

Mike was the kind of person who made his own laws, based on his own concepts, and at that time in his life, he was clearly capable of doing anything. I felt his violence like an inner volcano ready to erupt. He also had great charisma and leadership qualities. He could have become the leader of Hells Angels. When I told him that, he said, "You have no idea how right you are." For him, in his mentality at that time, good was only related to his opinions and desires. He was so centered and focused on himself and his needs that his vision of the world inflamed his rebellious side that was ready to impose his choices and decisions. I had rarely seen such energy, such power in a person. His father had a similar character. He could be impulsive, angry, bossy, even dictator-like sometimes, but his son was 100 times more powerful. The father was in the army and his father, Mike's grandfather, had committed suicide. That's why these parents had asked me to meet their son. They were terrified he would commit suicide and continue the family karmic chain. We can see here a generation focused on impulsivity, rigidity, duty, and a thirst for justice but which was constructed more on intolerance that on the good, humane, humanitarian side of the army and military service.

We walked along peacefully and I could feel that even walking slowly and peacefully was difficult for him; indeed, he didn't mind saying so in a sarcastic, scornful tone. When a person has too many negative memories and energy, he lives and experiences everything in extremes. It's one of the major characteristics of people on the edge of the abyss. Consequently they push and defy death in all sorts of ways, in extreme sport or behavior, in exaggerated, competitive attitudes that can kill relationships, friendships, etc. As we walked along and talked, I could feel that Mike wasn't aware of the depths of my analysis.

It is very important to use our angelic powers, our clairvoyance, clairsentience and clairaudience in such a way that the other person doesn't feel our extra-sensorial perceptions. We must be neutral and humble with our multi-dimensional discernment, and above all, never dramatize or be afraid for his life or for ourselves. During the course of my life, I've met several criminals, schizophrenics, and people who've told me about violent acts they committed, and each time I welcomed them with love and kindness, never making any difference between them and others. Mike felt that and knew that I appreciated him, that I didn't only see his weakness, but that I could also see his tremendous potential.

For me, a person going through difficulties is a soul *in the making*, a soul in mutation. There are no dramatizing dynamics in me regarding negativity or evil. I know that Divine Justice is rigorous with those who decide to experiment the paths of evil and wrongdoing, hurting themselves and others. However, I also see such choices as evolutive experimentations that, one day, will lead the person to understand that he has not chosen the right path, that the purpose of Divine Rigor and Justice is precisely that, and not at all condemnation for all eternity! I know that one day each and every one of us will achieve Enlightenment, we will all find the Light. For me that is absolutely clear, even though it may take several, or even many lives. I understand both victim and aggressor. I know they attract each other like magnets because they have things to learn and understand from each other. I know that a victim today was once an aggressor in another life. Hence through his encounter with an aggressor, he actually encounters himself. Knowing that we have to protect, help, and feel great compassion for victims, knowing that it is necessary to imprison those who commit serious crimes so they can have some time to reflect on what they did and cleanse their destructive forces and memories, I also know that such karmic cycles can and do end. Integrating this knowledge really helps us not to dramatize evil and not to nourish such distorted energies. It is also possible to encounter aggressor-victim aspects in our dreams and work on ourselves to cleanse these aspects without necessarily having to go through difficult ordeals in our concrete current life.

In simple language he could understand, I spoke to Mike about the psychology of Angels, about everyone's potential to develop their inner faculties, to purify and cleanse their memories using Angel Mantra Recitation. Although he had always refused his parents' spiritual approach, I felt him opening to me, and with new enthusiasm, he spontaneously said, "I've got an idea! I could go on a 4-day retreat in a monastery!" I told him that if he felt an inner calling to do so it might be the right decision for him. He added, "I'm going to borrow *The Book of Angels, The Hidden Secrets* from my parents and I'll read it during my retreat." And off he went happy, with renewed positive energy. Throughout our conversation, I had filtered his vital energy by constantly invoking Angel 14 Mebahel, whose Divine Qualities are:

ANGEL 14 MEBAHEL

* Commitment
* Humanitarian aid, altruism
* Motto: Truth, Liberty, and Justice
* Unconditional love
* Inspiration from Higher Worlds
* Liberates the oppressed and prisoners
* Helps those who have lost hope
* Equity, likes accuracy, re-establishes natural order
* Respectful conduct toward the environment
* Exorcism
* Mediation
* Wealth, elevation of the senses

Human Distortions related to Angel 14 Mebahel

• *Lack of commitment*
• *Does not keep promises*
• *Feeling of being disliked, unloved, rejected*
• *Diabolical forces, inner struggle*
• *Lies, false testimony*
• *Lawsuits, accusations, captivity, oppression, slander*
• *Usurpation, adversity, law-breaker, criminal*
• *Tyrant and victim*
• *Identifies with social laws*
• *Goes against the tide*

I could see his energy had totally changed. This glimmer of hope was another angelic miracle. He did go to the monastery, and one night when he prayed and asked for divine help, I visited him in a dream. *I was lying in bed meditating when his father came along and asked me to help his son. I agreed to help him. Another image followed wherein I saw Mike's father sitting anxiously but bravely dignified in this ordeal. Then I saw his mother who was very perturbed indeed, and her agitation made her much too emissive and incapable of helping her son. Mike was present too, sitting there with his fists tightly closed, shaking and trembling all over. I went over to the washbasin and filled a glass with water and offered it to Mike. After a little hesitation, he accepted the glass of water and drank it. Then I found myself in a kitchen. Up on the highest shelf there were loud-speakers emitting extremely aggressive, almost demonic music; it was really very powerful. I climbed up on a stool to turn down the volume. I eventually managed to turn it down although it was difficult as the music was so powerful and demonic to show me just how powerful the negative ambiances in this young man were.*

Then another sequence of images continued the dream. *I saw myself talk to Mike. He told me he greatly admired his father,* who had made a career for himself in the Canadian army. Then *I saw Mike standing beside a distributor of energy drinks for sports people,* which indicated that now, relieved by the decrease in volume of the demonic sounds in his head, he could continue his inner work by activating intense emotional, sporting energies; hence he could learn to channel and transform his aggression through sport. Then, a final scene *showed me the young man following in his father's footsteps, joining the Canadian army.*

A few days later, on his return from the monastery, his parents contacted me to tell me their son had come back radiant; he had re-discovered his joie de vivre. He'd told them, "I feel liberated, no more dreadful thoughts spinning in my head." Without revealing my dream, I suggested that it might be good for their son to enroll in the Canadian army. It would help give him an aim in life, and the training would help him manage his inner forces. I discreetly kept total silence about the angelic work I had done, and months later, I received the good news that Mike had been accepted for officer training in the Canadian army. He had decided to follow in his father's footsteps and have a military career. I was also very moved when years later, Mike's family invited me to attend his graduation.

All these years, and still today, Up Above has allowed me to continue to follow Mike in my dreams. From time to time, I help him without his knowing. Maybe one day he will read this book and find out, but if so, he will be ready to know it then. I've always known he had tremendous potential in spite of all the detours he may have followed in order to become who he is today. After our meeting, he went through other ordeals, but managed to come through them and regain the pathway of his life program. Several interventions in the Parallel Worlds were necessary, and not only by me, but Mike evolved and today he is much better.

Unlike the man I cured of cancer, Mike's parents began to help others and are actively involved in humanitarian projects. His father has now retired from the army. His mother is a prison warden in a juvenile penitentiary for murder cases and other serious criminal offences. Both parents now do voluntary work to help people. Their radiance and influence are exemplary and inspire a lot of people. They succeeded in getting themselves out of their family karma because they prayed and asked the Angels for help. The work I did could have been done by someone else. It just happened to be my responsibility, and hence I too was able to learn and grow angelically. It is important to always do this kind of work unconditionally, and never to consider ourselves indispensible or unique. There are thousands of angelic guides in the Parallel Worlds watching over us, thereby continuing their own personal evolution too. Whenever we help a person, we learn; we always receive great Teachings.

41. The O.J. Simpson Trial

From 1995 to 1997, the criminal and civil trials of O.J. Simpson related to the murder of his wife were detailed in all of the USA newspapers and media. At that time, I was in my retreat period there, studying and working day and night on the development and integration of my angelic conscience. World opinion was scandalized to see that legal niceties had led to O.J. Simpson being acquitted of his wife's murder in spite of all the evidence presented in court. As for me, I had no particular point of view, nor indeed any interest in following the case. I heard about it from time to time on the news, of course. It was the period in my life when I was studying world events in the Parallel Worlds, in my dreams. It was when Carolyn and her husband Tim had so kindly provided me with lodgings in exchange for some gardening and help in their house in Cold Springs. I still remember the stunned look on Carolyn's face when she found me sorting through newspaper cuttings all related to major world events. She left the room without saying anything, and we never discussed the subject thereafter. At that time, all of my dreams and notes on the interventions I'd carried out related to world events were stored in a special file that I always kept with me. I no longer do this, but at that period in my life, this helped convince me, and taught me deeply that everything I experienced in dreams was truly real.

So the night before February 6th, 1997, the night before the verdict of the civil court was to be pronounced, and after visiting O.J. in dreams several times over the previous two years, *I found myself in a room with him. I was dressed in white. He was sitting there and he looked up at me with great fear in his eyes. With deep, loving kindness and rigor, I said to him, "That's enough, now. The veil is about to be lifted."* Knowing that the verdict was to be pronounced the following day, I turned on the TV and was able to watch the live proceedings of his condemnation. A verdict of guilty was pronounced.

That event and several others like it completely transformed my conception of human consciousness because, yes indeed, I saw myself take action in dreams that had a real impact on Earth and in people's lives. Moreover, especially in the beginning, I had no idea what was going to happen, what could happen, as I hadn't even particularly wanted to do or say such a thing, behave in such a way, etc. I'd just found myself doing so in the dream.

When we start to experiment our angelic powers, in our dreams, we may find ourselves in situations where we act with divine conscience even though our conscience is not yet divine on the concrete, physical level. In dreams, we can see ourselves take action, do things, help, heal, etc., as if we knew how to, as if we knew everything there was to know, whereas, in actual fact, most of the time, we know nothing at all, or very little. I didn't want to condemn O.J. Simpson. I hadn't taken sides at all because it was impossible for me to know if he really was guilty or not. However, in dreams, it's quite a different matter. When we are given access to the collective program, we develop a kind of omniscience. Hence Divine Will can be conveyed through us, inspire us, connect us to God's Conscience, God's Cosmic Computer, and show us through symbols what is going on, or what will occur in the near or distant future. With time, our conscience is transformed and we use our angelic powers consciously. One day, we can even have a lucid dream while meditating and enter the Cosmic Computer to check what is going on, and consequently act on Earth in accordance with the information received. We can have access to the past, present and future, or to the probabilities of what is in preparation. Our angelic powers are immense! The more we work on ourselves with Angel Mantra Recitation, the more we integrate the Divine Qualities, the more our spiritual powers grow in us. And as they grow, so too does our responsibility.

Angel work leads us to understand the Divine collective plan, and the interaction between good and evil. We learn to see good and evil as active forces of evolution that are natural and normal in the process of human development. We become more aware of Divine Justice. Angel work gradually leads us to be completely neutral, and to have love and compassion for everything that exists. It also helps us cleanse our interferences and limiting concepts. In another chapter of this book, I will share with you one of the initiations that led me to receive my universal passport, giving me access in real time to the Universal Library, called *Daath* or *Akashic Memories,* which contains all knowledge of Humanity.

42. No More Seduction

Some time after my separation from the mother of my child, I shared a mountain chalet with a dental surgeon friend of mine. He too had just separated from his wife and was going through a difficult period. He and I were very different. I was more solitary, always interiorizing and praying, whereas he got through his pain by exteriorizing, going boating, being continually active. At the same time we remained friends, and still are friends today, even though we don't see each other very often.

One evening, all sunny smiles, he happily told me, "I've got a date this evening!" And very sure of himself, he added, that he probably wouldn't be home that night, at least, he hoped not. Knowing that the re-construction of his soul wasn't yet complete, that he was still suffering and emotionally was all mixed up and confused, I looked him in the eye and asked, "Are you sure that's a good idea? Do you love this woman enough to spend the rest of your life with her?" He was well aware of my morals and ethics regarding relationships and replied a little vaguely, slightly sarcastically, with a hint of rebellion, "It's true I don't love her but life is to be enjoyed, isn't it? There's no harm in having fun." And off he went proud of his declaration, knowing that I would remain in my room. Even though he liked and respected me a lot, in his eyes, I was too reserved. He thought I was on a slightly excessive path.

That night, without wanting to, I found myself in a dream where *I was dressed all in white, standing near a house where the window had actually been removed. While remaining outside, I had access to a bedroom, and I saw my friend begin lovemaking. The woman's energy was less present than his. I saw myself raise my hand and shine Light onto his body and into the room.* The following morning he arrived home in a good mood as usual. He was a person who always had a very positive philosophy about everything. He was a beautiful soul in spite of his slightly superficial side. He often wore a mask of success and unwavering strength. I was meditating in the garden and he came to greet me as usual. He sat on the tire that served as a swing and I told him my dream about him. He started to laugh and laugh and laugh good heartedly. He told me that during intercourse, while everything seemed to be going well, all of a sudden, he lost his erection, instantaneously, as fast as lightning, so fast, he didn't understand what had happened. "It's the first time that has ever happened to me," he said. "I was so embarrassed." And he laughed wholeheartedly at the thought that I had visited him at that particularly intimate moment.

43. The Birth of my Nephew

The more I experimented all sorts of things, the more confident I became in what we can all become, in what we can all do with our angelic conscience. I wrote down all of my dreams, and made a note of all of the angelic work I did, which I read and re-read, and meditated on, turning each experience over and over in my head in an effort to understand the slightest detail, to understand how it all worked. My sister and I are especially close. She was my first student, one of the first people I helped in a dream, in the Parallel Worlds. With 10-50 dreams per night, as well as all my lucid dreams, I can assure you I did, and continue to do, my flight-hours! I sometimes feel like an airplane pilot with a very full logbook!

When my niece, Ariel Mikaël, and my nephew, Gabriel Menadel (my sister, Nathalie, and my brother-in-law, Jean, gave both of them Angel names) were born, I was able to attend the birth and accompany them in dreams, while Christiane, my wife, was actually present in the labor ward. Once again, I hadn't asked to see the birth in a dream; I just found myself there in my dream the night my sister gave birth.

Let me share with you how this happened for my nephew, Gabriel Menadel. While his mother gave birth to him in hospital, I saw him in a dream. *I saw him arrive on Earth already quite old; he wasn't just a baby, he was a child of about 7 or 8 years old. I felt he had great potential, immense sensitivity. I saw him fall into a glass of milk and he was scared of being drunk by his father.* By the time I received this dream, I already understood symbolism well and I knew I had been shown his program, the outlines of what he would have to go through, what he needed to transcend to develop and grow to his full potential.

The fact that he was older than normal showed that he would always be in advance, that he would always be very mature for his age, and that is still the case today, at the age of 9. He has always been precocious in everything, and is a lot like I used to be. He is allergic to cow's milk and all sorts of pollen and other allergens. He is also asthmatic. This dream showed that he was so receptive he penetrated people by becoming a liquid, which meant that emotionally (liquid=emotions) he could sometimes be in such symbiosis with others that he would lose his personality in them. The presence of his father was not solely related to Gabriel's own father, but rather to concrete action and behavior because a father symbolizes action, concrete materialization. Hence, as a result of this hypersensitivity, this spiritual aspect (because milk is white and white=spirituality), Gabriel's clairsentience would be very strong, so strong that he would penetrate other people's energy without realizing at first.

And indeed, this child's sensitivity is phenomenal! Receptivity is one of the great characteristics of these new children who continually guess ahead of themselves and others and fuse with them, a little like *E.T.* the extraterrestrial in Steven Spielberg's film, who just like a sponge, becomes and feels all that his friend Elliot experiences. Gabriel is like that and I too was like that when I was young: allergic to everything and very sensitive. I did all I could to ensure other people were happy, to please them, to make them laugh, etc. I had multiple personalities, changing from one minute to the next. Depending on who I was with, I became the other person. I answered or expressed their unconscious. I became an accelerating factor in their evolution and experimentation. I astonished myself at times. If I was with an intellectual person, I became more intelligent. I'd use advanced, elaborate vocabulary that I'd never used or even heard of before. And if people found me ordinary, if people didn't have confidence in me, then I lost my self-confidence and self-esteem. Oof! It took me a long time to gain stability. Just writing about this reminds me of the confused, mixed up, unstable, fragile, and simultaneously wonderful childhood I had. I see a lot of myself in Gabriel, that's for sure, and indeed, in all of the new children today, all of those beautiful angels in the making.

44. The Village Sages

After the dream I'd had about King Solomon and my encounter with the bookstore owner who'd offered to give my number to Christiane, I heard that meditations were held in the store every week. At that time in my life, I was perplexed and uncomfortable with people on the spiritual level, in a world where all of my spiritual experiences were well veiled and kept secret. Nevertheless, I accepted his invitation to come along to the meditations that were held 2-3 times a week, if I remember rightly. Although uncomfortable, I was also fascinated to meet the village sages. I told myself it would be wonderful, that surely they would be able to help me solve my enigmas, my dreams, my great questioning. I had never done any meditation or read any spiritual books in my life, so I was expecting to discover an extraordinary new world. My expectations were very high, I must admit. I was really hoping for answers from these meditations. I hadn't realized that I actually had been meditating since early childhood!

Off I went to the first session, which took place a short time before I began giving energy healings, and I'll never forget that first time. We were all sitting in the center of the bookshop, surrounded by books, surrounded by knowledge, and I was very embarrassed as well as very reserved and interiorized. I observed everyone there and I was impressed to meet these village sages. It was wonderful for me to get to know them. I studied and analyzed them as fast as a top speed computer that picks up and integrates every thought, every gesture, every movement so as to decode the mysteries, the slightest electron, ion, and atom of knowledge! Sitting in a circle, we all held hands as spiritual music played softly in the background. I didn't know what kind of meditation it was, but I had gathered it was a healing meditation. That suited me fine since I really needed to be healed. I kept asking God to heal me, to purify me, to help me become a better soul. As I already mentioned, I was very intense at the beginning; I was like a wild horse no one could ride. I was constantly alert and on the look-out regarding everything. I was a bit of an extremist too. At one point, the meditation leader announced, "Now, we are going to send healing energy to Stephany." Everyone sent energy to heal Stephany, but I started to weep in silence, apologizing on the inside, saying, "God, I'm sorry, I can't send Stephany healing energy; I've hardly got any for myself. I'm so sorry. I promise I'll do it when I'm better, when I've healed my memories. I'm not advanced enough. I'm not as advanced as these wise people here. I'm so sorry, please forgive me." And I cried and cried and apologized from the depths of my heart and soul.

When this meditation ended I was full of respect for these village sages. I didn't speak much, I was still in a sacred mood and attitude. It was very solemn, and I felt honored to be among them. They invited me to join them and share some time together over a meal in a local restaurant. And in the restaurant, I was deeply disappointed. I heard them criticize each other. I saw them choose ordinary, rather unhealthy food. I was stunned by the contrast between the wonderful time I'd had in the bookstore meditating in their company, wanting to heal Stephany and the world, and here in the restaurant, where they didn't apply even the most basic Laws of wisdom and respect. I saw some of them being too affectionate. One man put his arms around a woman, and he kept hugging her tightly while her husband sitting nearby seemed to think this was a beautiful gesture of unconditional love. I could feel it was far from divine. The man was clearly nourishing his basic instincts, his ego, his need for power, for acknowledgement. I didn't stay very long as I too was being judgmental and extreme. As soon as I could, I returned to take refuge in my hermit's chalet. However, I did go back to the meditations and I began to experiment energy.

During meditation, the group used to hold hands and they always circulated energy clockwise. As an experiment, without saying anything, I tried circulating the energy in the other direction to see what would happen. I also intensified it so much that some people were taken aback. I didn't say anything about my experimentation, and afterwards everyone would talk about how special the energy circulation had been that day. Of course, I now realize it wasn't right for me to do that, but in my extreme energy I wanted to help them purify themselves more, and since I had just started working with Angels at that time, I sent them Angel Energies. In addition to this, when I accompanied them to the restaurant, I tried to talk about what I was going through, the knowledge I was seeking, but I could feel it was too much for them; they didn't like my kind of questions. I was convinced they had answers that they wouldn't tell me, just like some of the priests and monks I'd encountered. Eventually, however, I realized that very often people pretend they have access to great knowledge, and use spirituality to obtain titles, become teachers, and above all to nourish their egos. Today it is impressive to see just how many therapists are more ill than their patients. Of course, there are also many good therapists, many wonderful people helping others, and more and more of these old New Age *dinosaurs* are being replaced by their children who do, or will do, things with deeper awareness and purer intentions. Very often, these children don't want their parents' spirituality. They find it far too airy-fairy. They think it belongs to La-La Land and is simply not plausible or valid. And they are absolutely right. True spirituality, in my opinion, is to develop Qualities, Virtues and Divine Powers.

45. Stage Fright

Several years went by and I was now married to Christiane and working with her, preparing lectures. I didn't really want to share my knowledge publically, so I helped and transmitted my angelic knowledge to Christiane, who then shared it in lectures. How did we work? First, Christiane would prepare her lecture, and then she'd show it to me. Then, I would deepen certain aspects, adding information, teachings and deep understandings I had received in dreams. Today, we still form a wonderful, dedicated work team devoted to the angels, except that nowadays I have very little to add to these lectures as my wife has integrated her angelic conscience and joyfully radiates it with all the love and purity of her heart and soul. It is a real blessing for us to have grown together as a couple, to have journeyed together with angelic knowledge to become who we are today. Angel Teaching truly leads to spiritual autonomy. Invoking Angels is very, very powerful.

At first, I didn't give any lectures, but very gradually, I began sharing during the workshops we gave. One of the first workshops I led was also a great learning experience, and it helped me develop a wiser way of transmitting angelic and symbolic knowledge. We had included a lecture by me in the workshop program. Christiane did most of the teaching and I had a shorter section. This was my choice because I didn't feel ready to do more. Besides, Christiane taught so well, as indeed she continues to do so today. Once or twice I had tried to share during one of Christiane's lectures, but in front of a room full of people, with my level of receptivity, I could feel the slightest skepticism, the slightest rejection. I couldn't de-focus my attention from these negative thoughts, and I'd become a bit of a simpleton, incapable of speaking well, unable to transmit my knowledge clearly and coherently. I very quickly became aware of this because I had had the same problem as a young artist, when a TV or radio presenter wasn't in symbiosis with me in an interview, I lost interest. In fact, I embodied his lack of interest in the subject, and so it was difficult for me to talk and express myself clearly. This lack of emissivity has now been rectified, but oh! it took me a long time to understand my sensitivity. Today, it is one of my greatest strengths, but it took years for it to stabilize.

For the workshop, which included a lecture by me, I'd had the idea that during the night, in my dreams, I could visit each person present, and I could then share with them what I had seen. I was sure that they'd be happy to hear about themselves so I spent the night visiting all of them. The following afternoon, after Christiane's wonderful lecture, when it was my turn to share, I started to explain my workshop and one by one, I began to reveal what I had seen in my dreams about each person. Oops! Everyone went all stiff and silent, and I realized that I shouldn't have revealed so much information even though I knew it was right and true. It only took one experience like this to serve as a lesson for me. It still serves me today, and it will serve me for the rest of my life.

Needless to say, nothing dreadful happened, it remained on the subtle levels. Just by the stiffer posture, the ever so slight withdrawal, I could feel the person closing rather than opening, and I understood the importance of spiritual autonomy, of each person receiving his teachings personally through his own dreams and his signs, which is the very core of our teaching today. After this experience, I decided to show people how to use Angel Energies to learn how to live angelically, how to become angels, how to receive their own answers, rather than give them the answers. Spiritual autonomy is the foundation, the very cornerstone of our teaching, and Christiane and I have devoted and continue to devote our lives to fulfilling our deepest, heartfelt wish, to carrying out our Mission, which is to help people learn and develop their spiritual autonomy, to help them grow their own wings.

46. There is No Mistake

Making mistakes while experimenting in order to learn is not easy. It requires a lot of humility to work on ourselves, and even more so when we work with Angels, with Divine States of Conscience. The angelic capacities that are activated in us are very powerful and they introduce us to the World of Truth. When we understand and speak symbolic language, we have access to the archetypal level of ourselves, of others, and the whole Universe. However, visiting ourselves is the basis of this work. We can rest assured that the Cosmic Computer, God and His Angels, constantly supervise the actions of the guides and travelers in the Parallel Worlds. The police Up Above are even more rigorous than on Earth, that's for sure! If we haven't got permission to go somewhere, the program won't work, we won't be able to go there; unless, of course, we are sent there to learn something.

One thing we also come to understand with time and through experimenting is that there is no such thing as a mistake. We are all trying things out, testing ourselves in order to evolve, unconsciously for much of the time, but with an angelic conscience too. We have to experiment, to learn deeply, to improve ourselves and become better people, better souls. If we do make a *mistake*, if there is an *error*, then it's because there was a reason for it; it was intended to happen on the Cosmic level; the error was permitted. Otherwise, we receive an inspiration or intuition and we do something to avoid the error. And even though freedom of choice, our free will, is always favored, we can even become robots for Heaven if Up Above so wishes. Our misactions – an apparently wrong turn or poor timing, for example – may have been orchestrated to prevent an ordeal and help us evolve more easily, or to ensure that we meet and help someone else evolve. We always receive guidance, and just as children are helped and guided by their parents, we too can be helped avoid errors that would have too great a consequence for our future. As we don't yet know what we are to become, we are *remote-controlled*, so to speak, to ensure we head in the right direction for our program, our life plan. *There is no mistake* is a fascinating concept to meditate on, to integrate. We can add *there are only experimentations!*

47. What if I Drown?

Once I was in the world of dreams, in the Parallel Worlds, and *as a guide and I were swimming, I shared my impressions with him. I told him how fascinated I was by the tangible feel of the water. I told him it was identical to water on Earth. There was no difference between swimming in the sea on Earth and swimming with him in this water in the Parallel Worlds. Then I asked him a question. "But what if I stop swimming, what happens here? Will I go under and drown?" He replied with deep wisdom and experience, "Yes, you'll go under and drown, but you'll automatically transfer to another World."* I woke up delighted and amazed once again by this astral voyage.

What he had told me made such good sense because death is simply a passageway. There is no real, ultimate death, only physical death. The spirit lives on; it leaves its physical envelope behind and instantaneously changes dimension. Needless to say, we should never play around with death. If you intend to commit suicide in order to see what is on the other side, you won't find yourself in a beautiful world. Oh no! Not at all! You will end up in a world that corresponds to what was in your heart and mind. Life is sacred and must be respected at all times and in all circumstances. Wanting to know too much can be one of the worst dangers for your soul. Let teachings and experience come gradually to you, and don't forget the aim of the *game* of life is to discover the rules of good and evil.

48. What Name Do You Want?

Once in another dream at the beginning of my opening, *I met one of the guides of the Parallel Worlds for the first time. I was so moved I burst into tears and sobbed my heart out, thanking him for being there. He was dressed quite ordinarily; it was as if he worked for an electricity company, and he had come to the house.* Can you imagine being so happy when a technician comes to help you with the electricity that you burst into tears and begin to sob as you thank him for coming! He would surely look at you quizzically to say the least, while probably inwardly saying to himself, 'What a strange reaction! This person seems weird!' Well, that's exactly how the guide looked at me. I could read his thoughts and see he was saying to himself, 'He's got a problem with his emotions.' *Once I had managed to calm my over-happy emotions, I asked him his name, and he replied with a question: "What name do you want?"* And I woke up with this dream that had been so real, as real as concrete reality.

I thought about this question for days. "What name do you want?" Lots of people receive the name of their guide in a dream, or they hear a name or voices telling them, and they turn this name into an icon and bestow it with all sorts of apparent powers and possibilities, whereas fundamentally, that name is purely symbolic, representing a part of their conscience, an aspect of their personality. If a person in a dream tells you her name is Carmine, then you need to ask yourself what Carmine represents for you. If a person you know is called Carmine, then there is a link with this person's behavior and attitude. However, the fact that the Carmine you know in concrete reality didn't feature in the dream means that this dream reveals aspects of you, and was not a visit to this person's soul. On the other hand, if the name in the dream is unknown to you, Nathael, for instance, and you don't know anyone of that name, then in your dream you are either encountering new behavior and attitudes that you don't yet know you have, or discovering a new type of of influence or personality, a new program that has been activated in your inner computer.

It is important to understand this phenomenon. Lots of people now dream of myself, my wife, Christiane, my daughter Kasara, Anthony, or other teachers of our school. Each time, the person must refer back to himself, and ask, 'What does this person represent for me?' Usually we are spiritual symbols, representing evolution, Angel work, angelic living, the angelic path; hence our presence in these dreams shows the dreamer how his own spiritual parts behave. Some people think that when they dream of me I must have come to visit them in the dream, but that is not always the case. Guides from the Parallel Worlds can easily take on my likeness in order to convey a message to the dreamer, and just like my swimming experience, "I" may seem very real in the dream, as tangible as in concrete reality. Hence, some people are absolutely sure they met me in their dream while I have no memory at all of such an encounter.

112

As a therapist it is essential never to use dreams to take other people's power; for instance, when one of your patients tells you he dreamed about you. In such a case I always tell them it's not important that it was me; what is important is to analyze this symbol as part of themselves, because that's the whole point of dreams. Through the interaction of all the symbols present, dreams convey messages and teachings for the good of our soul's evolution, to help us develop qualities, virtues, and become better people. If I have actually visited the person in a dream, and if I feel the person is testing me to see what I will say, if I think he was impressed by my presence in his dream, or trying to give me his power, then I always refer the dream and my presence in it back to the dreamer, either not saying anything at all about the visit, or denying it, saying I hadn't visited him, even if I had. I don't go all mysterious and cast my eyes down. I prefer to seem less important than to weaken the dreamer's own capacities. It is all-important that people keep their powers and develop them themselves. Very rarely do I reveal my angelic work; this book is quite unique for me. There is a lot of hitherto unpublished subject matter in this biography, which I have written for the sole purpose of helping all those who wish to discover work with the Angels on Earth. I am convinced this testimonial will help a lot of people as well as future generations to better understand the true meaning of what an angel is.

CHAPTER SIX
THE HIDDEN LIFE

This chapter *The Hidden Life* explains the result of long, deep reflection on how to behave with others in society when we live with angelic powers. Kaya's decision not to reveal, but to keep hidden, how he lived came about gradually after some difficult experiences with the media. Later he decided to wait more than 12 years before giving any media interviews again. This unique, extraordinary book reveals for the first time in 18 years, what he is, what he has become through his work with the Angels.

49. From FM to K

I was becoming more and more aware of the need for me to change my life. The more my unconscious opened, the more I felt that there was no longer any need for my former self. I didn't, and don't, deny what I was. On the contrary, I was very much aware that life is a path, a journey, a story with a beginning, a middle, a conclusion, a new beginning, and so on. Most of the time, though, people don't begin again in the same life. Unless we become spiritual, unconsciously, most of us wait for the next life to start afresh.

Angelic living led me to a completely different perception of everyday life and living. For me, all that mattered was to develop Divine Qualities, to become a better soul, and to continue to learn, to help, and to heal in the Parallel Worlds. I lived as a recluse, spending more and more time in prayer. Such a lifestyle came naturally to me; it was as though it was my true identity. Since I hadn't read many books nor been exposed to many different world cultures, I didn't know that in many spiritual traditions, when a person commits to a religious life, he changes his name; he takes on a new identity. This has been so since time immemorial. For Tibetan monks, Christian priests and nuns, in Islam and other religious, spiritual traditions, it is customary to take on a new identity when committing oneself to serve Heaven on Earth. I now understand this phenomenon, the feeling of needing to turn the page and start afresh, because as soon as our spiritual conscience is activated, we encounter new perceptions, which completely transform our way of living, our very existence. You really need to have felt this spiritual calling to know what I mean. People who haven't experienced this tend to scorn and ridicule and find it difficult, even impossible, to understand spiritual people journeying on a deep, intense path. It's like having a job that doesn't make us happy – we may have decided to do it only to please our father or mother – and all of a sudden, we decide to *recycle* our life, to change our job or career orientation, and go toward something that truly pleases us. Today, after all my mutations of conscience, I truly understand what change is! I also have deep compassion for homosexuals who may find themselves cast aside, rejected, misunderstood, and sometimes banished from their clan, from their family because of their difference.

Being born under the star of change is quite a program. That is why, wanting to realize my mystical flame, feeling a calling to materialize, to embody this angelic mutation, I decided to take on a new name, a *nom de plume*, an author's pseudonym or pen name, and to set aside Francis Martin, the artist's name I had adopted at that time, which no longer suited me at all. I could no longer identify with that person I had created, that everyone knew. The

Francis Martin that people knew was nothing like the real me, and nothing like the new person I had become. Francis Martin was more of an artistic mask, a role I had played and shaped over time as a result of always keeping my spirituality hidden deep within me. Today, of course, I don't advise anyone to change their name when they experience their angelic awakening. It isn't necessary because it can cause far too much upheaval in their life and even create insurmountable problems for some. During the complete transformation of my life, I was indeed protected by Up Above, because I could so easily have gotten completely lost.

When a person becomes a Tibetan monk, for instance, he enters a world of traditional customs, rituals, and an ordered, regulated lifestyle, all of which help him accept the change more easily. I wasn't affiliated to any particular religion or movement. I was alone on my spiritual path, which made it all the more difficult for people to understand. And when you are a star in the music world, a social and collective symbol identified with hit songs, multi-million dollar contracts, and a lifestyle almost everyone dreams of, it really isn't easy to publically change your name and be understood by materialistic, worldly people, some of whom would give anything to be in your shoes, to live your life of abundance, and to have your stardom, your radiance that opens all sorts of doors so easily.

At first, my name change was simply a pen name that would draw a veil over and hide who I had been. I didn't think that I would become even more popular than I had been, but today books published under the name of Kaya are now available in over 43 countries in the world. I had no concrete idea of what was to happen regarding my future, only dreams predicting it that I found difficult to believe. My path was very personal and by changing my name, I stepped aside and walked away, leaving stardom aside to once again become anonymous and more humble in order to begin a new cycle of existence in the same life.

The first time the name Kaya came to me was during a meditation and this name just came to mind quite naturally. I hadn't been seeking a new name in meditation; I hadn't been thinking about it at all. It was as if a new program had been activated in my head and a new piece of information inserted. I was so surprised the first time I received this totally unpremeditated idea. It just flashed into my mind. At first, it was James Kaya Field but essentially it was only Kaya. Once again, although I knew Kaya was sufficient, given my tendency to mask my true identity, I had added James Field on either side of Kaya to protect myself, and to seem more concrete, less ethereal. Very quickly, though, it became simply Kaya. Immediately after the meditation, I sat down at the piano, and humming a tune, I composed a song in an unknown, inspired language, saying, *"Kaya co cété la sun… During my meditation, I received this information… Kaya co cété la sun… I saw a bright white light in the sky, talking to me."* After this, I received several dreams where I encountered guides and where I was called Kaya.

This major change caused shock waves throughout the whole of Quebec (Canada). I was ridiculed, scorned, misunderstood and considered crazy. It was very intense, and as I mentioned earlier, I became the butt of jokes and the number one public person to be ridiculed and laughed at daily on TV and radio shows. This went on for years and years; jokes were regularly made alluding to my spirituality. I understood everyone's reactions very well, and I accepted their judgments and criticism. I couldn't explain this angelic mutation. I couldn't reveal the details of my inner life, all that I was experiencing on the inside. How could I have told people at that time what I've written in this autobiography today? My first book talked about it but without truly sharing because I constantly censored each word, veiling the deep aspects, not telling how I had lived since early childhood. Since then, many other books, co-written with my wife Christiane, have followed, setting in motion a new way of living, a new current of thought for mankind. They include *The Book of Angels, The Hidden Secrets; How To Read Signs, The Origin of the Traditional Study of Angels; Angelic Yoga, Introduction,* and several others.

The good thing is that, in the Western world, spirituality has evolved over the past 20 years; nowadays it is easier to share more openly, and to open up new paths of evolution. Today, I can also say in all humility that the fact of having been scorned and ridiculed for years and years was one of the greatest evolutive gifts I ever received. It allowed me to discover, build, and fortify unsuspected strengths in me, to develop detachment, to cleanse mockery within

118

myself, to develop extraordinary, unconditional love for all human beings. I can assure you that if you work with the Angels, invoking Them every day, you too will experience initiations where you will have to transcend scorn, humiliation, the anxious, limitative 'What will people say?', all that worrying about what people may think and say about you. You won't necessarily have to go through all this in public like I did, but you need to know that in order to activate high states of conscience of love and wisdom, we are shaken right to the very depths of our whole being: body, mind, heart and soul. Mockery is one of the states of conscience that we have to transcend in order to accede to high levels of conscience. To truly follow our dreams and guidance, to be able to obey our higher nature in all circumstances, to incarnate God's Will, to marry spirit and matter, we need to surpass and transcend the need to please, to be loved, appreciated, complimented, flattered by others. Such needs erode our courage, obscure our vision and understanding, and lead to our being bogged down and mired in non-evolutive behavioral patterns. I can assure you that my great public humiliation helped me grow so much! Moreover, when I set this great change of life in motion, I was well aware of the impact it would have in the society where I had grown up in fame since childhood. I saw what was going to happen in dreams, and at the same time, I was told *it was necessary but that I was going to be protected, that our Heavenly Father was going to help me.* However, in spite of this reassurance, I cried my heart out. I prayed and cried, and cried and prayed before undertaking this change and making it public. In the beginning I felt so lost!

I remember a meeting I had with my first editor. He published my first book *Equilibrium,* before Christiane and I founded our non-profit organization Universe/City Mikaël (UCM). He was very nice to me. He told me that his wife was spiritual, that she had read my book, and that he appreciated the step I was taking since he himself was a member of Alcoholics Anonymous; he too had undergone great changes in his own life regarding the man he had been. I will always remember how kind and open he was with me. In his great big office in Montreal that radiated success and abundance, he looked me in the eye and asked, "Are you aware of what you are going to reveal, and what it will do to your life?" I told him that I was, that I'd had dreams telling me that one day my example would help millions of people, but that it would be very difficult at first; I was aware of that. I reassured him that he didn't need to worry about me. I had received a large inheritance so I didn't have to worry about my basic needs, and I knew that if things didn't go well, then I'd simply retire from public life. He was speechless. Admiring my courage, he decided to support my initiative and publish that first book.

This first book was not very successful and soon became the butt of jokes. So much so that it was embarrassing for people to buy it. People didn't dare buy it for fear of seeming to agree with me, with what I was. Some people believed I was in a sect and dangerous. I was publically lynched on the radio phone-in shows that discussed the subject, judging and ridiculing me. It was intense, and in spite of front page publicity, the book hardly sold. People who had followed my career for years and years, the hundreds and thousands of people who had believed in me were all gone; I was alone. Even in spiritual circles, in esoteric bookstores, I was cast aside, feared, and rejected like the black sheep of the flock.

At first, I'd only opened my heart and shared a very simple message. I said that each and every one of us, no matter our religion or tradition, all of us had an inner world to discover. The message I shared was universal. It was meant to inspire people to open up to spiritual values. I didn't even mention Angels at the time. In spite of my message being a simple, modest, humble explanation that our sole purpose in life is to develop qualities, virtues and powers in their purest state, it was turned against me and became one of my greatest ordeals. God had told me in dreams that initially it would be difficult before my ability to help spiritually and to teach openly would emerge from this experience; but I didn't think it would be as difficult as it was.

50. The Value of Gold

In spite of the family and social turbulence I was going through, my hidden, unrevealed, angelic work and research continued, which helped me grow and mature. After 3-4 very intense weeks of media coverage, I chose to completely retire from the public eye and no longer give any interviews, which I did for more than 12 years. After this media experience, it was clear to me that the time had come to enter my *secret angel-agent* life. My social life had been sabotaged. I was no longer credible in most people's eyes. Henceforth, however, I could continue to serve Heaven and help Humanity anonymously. No one knew or believed in what I could do, and all the better. I understood that I now had more scope to do my initiatic work, to continue to improve myself, to develop and learn in silence. I was and still am, after almost 20 years of Angelic work in the Parallel Worlds, an eternal student. When we think we have reached the ultimate stage, another door opens, new Knowledge dazzles us, making us humble before the greatness that is God, Our Father, Our Mother, Our Creator. I have a lot of compassion for those who do not believe, who are atheists, who doubt what we can be, what we can become. At the same time, I understand them, because with my two feet firmly on the ground, my own faith was activated by the fact that I received proof, and went through amazing, extraordinary, mystical, transforming experiences. On the spiritual level, true experience can only come from yourself. That's why I always tell people, "Don't just take my word for it, test this for yourselves. Try invoking an Angel for 2-3 weeks and see if dreams are triggered or intensified. Receive your own answers in your dreams."

The more inner work we do, the more we cleanse our negative memories, the more access we are given to secrets, to premonitory dreams that can be very, very precise. In 2001, I saw in a dream *World headlines announcing in gold letters that the price of gold was going to soar to phenomenal heights. I even saw it was going to exceed 1500$ an ounce, whereas at that time it was only worth 255$ an ounce.* I was fascinated by such dreams that concerned materialization. They helped me evolve toward new amazing perspectives so as to be able to marry spirit and matter. I didn't doubt the information I received but I checked it. I followed the news to see if the dream was true on the concrete level, or if it simply referred to parts of me. We can easily confuse parts of ourselves, representing a defragmentation of our conscience, a visit to our own or the collective unconscious, with a real premonitory situation. At the beginning, we should always be very careful, even detached, from any result. At that time, matter and wealth was so unimportant to me that it never entered my head to use this information. In my mind, I had simply seen the information in a dream, but I hadn't been told to buy or invest in gold so this information was merely there to be studied and added to my collection of proof that it was indeed possible to receive precise information concerning material reality in our dreams.

Sometimes I even found myself reading documents locked away in safes or ultra-confidential government documents, etc. Never would it have crossed my mind to use this information for myself, or to cause harm in any way. I could have, but I knew that even just having an idea which Up Above did not want materialized, then I would simply have been de-programmed to forget it. Everything is possible. God really is all-powerful, and He only uses His powers for our good. Furthermore, the more we advance with an angelic conscience, the greater our desire to be right and just, to serve Humanity. This is what animates us and causes our soul to vibrate at the highest levels. Once we have really and truly integrated the fact that the sole purpose of life is to develop qualities and virtues, that our goal is to transcend matter, never to take, envy, or want what isn't ours, then we can live in peace, and I am now convinced that this is the only way to receive this kind of premonitory information.

If someone like Einstein openly revealed the fact that he received the $E=mc^2$ formula in a dream, you can be sure it was Heaven that allowed him to use it. Hence, we are consciously or unconsciously chosen and we continually receive information and guidance from the Superior Worlds. A businessman or an industrialist has a certain role to play in the movements of global capital markets, and, he is continually influenced positively or negatively; he follows his intuition or specialist analyses that may sometimes seem obvious to him. The higher the position we fill, the more crucial and essential a role information plays in helping us to decide well. Hence, to do their work, to make their collective decisions, such people have specialists and a huge network of contacts at their disposal here on Earth, but, simultaneously, they are also guided without their knowing it. Most people who have impressive collective destinies are they themselves surprised by the synchronicities and events that led them to their positions of power, that led them to the height of their art or fortune. Having been close to Celine Dion, I remember René, her agent and husband, Vito Luprano and her team, etc., and my own agent Ben Kaye, all telling me how flabbergasted they had been by the synchronicities and easy access to success. So much so that René became superstitious about the number 5, and still is to this day. Up Above gave him this sign, this symbol was put in place, and he has let himself be guided by this number for years and years. I also know that he was able to recognize destiny; he could feel it on the inside, and Celine very often had premonitory dreams. I listened to them talk about this over and over again; they were all dumbfounded by the forces of success that were activated in and around them. Even my co-manager, Vito Luprano, told me that he felt that one day I too would have access to this kind of synchronicity. He sensed it and spoke openly about it to me. He very often saw me in his dreams. At one point he even got annoyed and said that I was always in his head and he told me to stop coming to visit him in dreams at night. He was an intense person and I have only beautiful memories of the time we worked together.

51. The Stock Exchange in a Dream

Other people might have been strongly tempted to use this mystical information that I received in dreams, but as long as I hadn't been told, hadn't been instructed to do so, then I wouldn't have dared. God was so important for me and I had so much respect for God, for the Angels, that it was simply impossible for me to use such information without authorization. I also considered this kind of dream as a test for me to pass, as a temptation for me to vanquish, to transcend, symbolizing my capacity to raise my soul toward the highest levels of Knowledge. For years, all I asked the Angels for was purity. I had no desire to visit anyone nor to pointlessly enrich myself. Inwardly I knew that this was the way to obtain God's trust, the trust of *Big Boss* Himself. In a company, especially in a big company where there are various groups and hierarchies of power, very few people are capable of setting aside their personal ambitions. Some people who have no access to material powers may lack self-esteem, and this often keeps them safe from temptation, but timidity is not true transcendence.

It is very easy to see the stock exchange in a dream provided Up Above gives us access. Like Einstein, we can know what plans Cosmic Intelligence has for Earth well in advance. A company prepares and follows a 5-year plan, so just imagine what Up Above can do! In 1995, when the shares of CIBC, the Canadian bank, were worth around 15$, I saw a graph in a dream showing the future progression of those shares over several years. In 1996, they rose to 28.30$, in 1997 to 41.75$ and in 1998 to 59.80$. Recently, in 2012, they reached more than 80$, as well as paying dividends throughout these 16 years of growth. We are so small compared with Great Cosmic Intelligence, but great too since we have unlimited powers within ourselves to be discovered and developed. All that exists in the Universe exists within us.

52. The Open Book Dream

During these years of intense inner work and preparation, preparation, I remember a beautiful gift Cosmic Intelligence gave me in a dream. I was in the middle of great tumult and social rejection, and *I found myself rising up through the Universe in a column of Light, traveling at the speed of Light;* it was fascinating! At that time too I was told in another dream that I was a pioneer in these angelic experiences, that I was like Chris Hadfield, the first Canadian astronaut to walk in space, who went on his first flight in 1995. In the column of Light, the energy transports us, intensely aspiring us upward, while our whole body trembles. I often have this experience when I transfer to and from the Parallel Worlds, and I really love this kind of experience. *In that inter-world voyage, aspirated upward in that tunnel of magnificent, dazzling Light, I found myself in a room, a sort of organic, living place. I put my hand out and touched one of the walls. It was kind of sticky and yet not really sticky either; it had a gelatinous but non-sticky texture. My name appeared on the wall as I touched it and I was able to read my destiny, what I was going to become later on.* Let me tell you, not only did this sort of dream build and edify my conscience, it also gave me confidence to continue to advance, because as it was, I was advancing without any safety net, in total fusion, total trust in Up Above, as much in the mystical experiences as in what I was asked to do. Of course, I had to sort through and analyze what I was asked to do. It is essential to analyze all of our dreams symbolically, to examine and analyze the energy that talks to us to be sure that it is right, to evaluate and discern good from evil. Once in a dream, *a deceased woman asked me to contact her son, who was one of my friends. She was worried about him and wanted me to tell him she was alive and well, and that death didn't exist.* In the dream, *there was a sort of ladder and she was at the top of it. I had climbed up it to see and talk to her, and she'd made her request in a sad, worried, distraught voice.* When I woke up, I thought about it and I wondered, 'Why couldn't she go and tell her son herself? Why does she need me to do it for her?' I knew very well that my calling this teenage friend out of the blue to tell him "Your mother came to see and asked me to tell you she's alive and well so that you can believe in Heaven," would be totally weird and undoubtedly counterproductive. After pondering over this request and deciding not to follow it, I received other dreams that taught me that I should be vigilant regarding my access to the Parallel Worlds, that not everything should be revealed, that veils were necessary for some people, that illusion is educational, and that it was very important to respect it.

It's the same for this book. I know very well that some people will read it and not believe it, not understand the contents because their conscience is not ready or not sufficiently open for them to be able to integrate such reality. Inner connection is a very personal experience. However, I can assure you that in the near future, new technologies are going to appear – they are under construction at this very moment – and one day, we will have access to images and travel in the Parallel Worlds *via* our computers. Like astronauts, we'll be able to see in *reality-TV* what goes on in the parallel dimensions of the Universe, and hence receive Teachings and understandings that will transform our beliefs and way of living. I myself am thinking about whether or not I should get in touch with research laboratories and allow them to scan my conscience while dreaming and awake. I'm not yet sure if I will or not. I'm waiting for dreams about it. I'm certainly going to send them a copy of the new *Dictionary, The Source Code*, one of the projects of our foundation, which represents more than 15 years of research, and for the last 3 years, a team of more than 100 people, including doctors, nurses, teachers, therapists, etc., from several countries across the world worked on it. This wonderful collaboration allowed me to accelerate my work on the synthesis and definition of the symbolic language, which I am convinced will help generations of today and tomorrow. As well as *The Source Code*, we are currently working on books and dictionaries on various themes, including a symbolic approach to health and illness. Symbolic language is truly a key to understanding the other dimensions and our own terrestrial dimension because everything is symbolic and mathematical in the Universe. Everything is assembled and presented in terms of conscience, and represents qualities, virtues and powers either in their experimental stage, or in their pure state. I would be happy to collaborate with scientific laboratories to provide even more concrete proof, but I want to be sure to work with the right teams and not be used merely as a laboratory rat, nor do I want to transmit this knowledge to people who are not spiritual enough, or do not have the right intentions. I'll accept what Up Above decides. For me, dreams and symbols hold no secrets anymore. And one thing is sure, before I leave this planet, I'll do my best to leave behind as much knowledge as possible in as many forms as possible, *via* books, CDs, etc.

Another revealing, inspirational experience led me to consult my book of destiny in a dream. *My mother was at my side, although I knew it wasn't actually her but rather a symbol, a guide had taken on her form. I was able to consult the book of my destiny, my current destiny, which was in the making. I stood there turning the pages and I was aware that the pages were months, cycles of time and life. The pages were multi-dimensional and made of material that doesn't exist on Earth. It was as if the book were a computer, a magical but tangible framework. It was a wonderful sensation. Calmly and very respectfully, I turned the pages and was able to read my future, see my medium-term destiny. At the beginning, I turned and I turned pages and pages but there was nothing concrete for me for 3 years. Nothing would happen, there would be no activity for 3 years. I heard a voice, like a Computer voice say, "You are in advance of your program; there is nothing concrete in terms of projects for 3 years."* When I woke up, not only did I know that 3 symbolizes construction, one of the principle Qualities of Angel 3 Sitael, but I was also very happy to know I was in advance. I had meditated and worked so intensely to integrate Knowledge while living a hermit's life of solitude, it was encouraging to know all my work had been worthwhile, had helped me advance. I wasn't at all annoyed or put out by the fact that there was nothing concrete, no project to be undertaken even if before falling asleep, working with Angel Sitael, I had asked, "What Mission does God want me to accomplish? Apart from getting to know myself in depth, and helping and working in the Parallel Worlds – which suited me fine at that time – what is my Mission, please?" That had been my question and this dream was the reply. I was so happy because I had been told I was in advance, which also meant I had worked well, that I had done my *conscience homework* well, and passed my exams.

Having spent many months working solely on myself, without TV, radio or newspapers, I began to re-integrate the TV and use it to meditate, to cleanse whatever bothered or upset me, and to follow current affairs, which continued in dreams. It gradually became fantastic for me to listen to the news and then go and visit the situation in my dreams, or even act therein to support and help various life programs. These experiences were an integral part of my angel training, and over the years, I have become more and more experienced in this field, and I am happy to help and teach others how to gain access to and acquire these parameters of conscience and of life.

53. Accompanying the Deceased

The 6-year experience of communication with my grandfather as well as my childhood experiences of communication with spirits and entities meant that for me death and contact with deceased persons became, and remains, a normal part of my nights and metaphysical actions. One of my aunts, Aunt Janine, to whom I was very close, came to speak to me during the viewing of her body at the funeral home. I was sitting there in silence. My entire family was there and the majority of them hadn't seen me for a long time, as I lived as a recluse most of the time. Many of them didn't dare come over and talk to me and that suited me fine. Over time, I had learned to live with the fact that people feared me, and tended to reject or marginalize me even though I had done nothing wrong. It was my daily lot and good for my evolution. As time went by, I had noticed that this led to automatic sorting, and hence helped me not waste my time. Only spiritual people were kind enough to talk to me; other people didn't approach me. I could feel their eyes on me, their judgment and lack of understanding, and I kept working on myself to always be in a state of unconditional love.

So there I was sitting calmly in meditation, waiting for the funeral service that was shortly due to begin, when all of a sudden, I heard a voice in my head, seeming to speak through my voice, asking me, "Would you sing a song for me?" I replied, "Oh no, Aunt Janine, no songs, you know I've turned the page on music for the time being." She went on to ask me, "Well then, could you say something, maybe read a text? I'd love you to do that." I accepted her proposition, and only 5 seconds later, her daughter, Nicole, leaned over and whispered in my ear, "Would you read a text for us or maybe say something?" And, unsurprised, I replied, "Sure! I'd be very happy to." As I listened to the priest, I wondered what I could say because when he spoke about death, he was full of fear, ambiguity, and a lack of Knowledge. He wasn't very inspiring, and once again, I found myself measuring my words, not wanting to disturb anyone, trying to come up with words that wouldn't be too intense for the people attending the funeral. If I said I had just spoken to Aunt Janine, that she was really and truly present at that very moment, they would all have been frightened, even though it was her funeral service, and clear to me that it was only normal that she should be there herself. In the end, I made a rather timid, not very forceful speech, as I was used to doing. I preferred to come across as rather inane and insubstantial, than say things that weren't appropriate in the situation. Moreover, I wasn't a great orator at the time. I couldn't express well what I was going through.

I know there are a number of people who sometimes have psychic powers and who show them off to impress others and get attention. Most of the time, their powers are not very stable, nor is their deep intention very luminous. Such powers are more often than not a response to these people's egos, and they unwittingly become puppets of the low astral realms, of deceased people or manipulative entities, that may appear right at first only to ensnare them as time goes on. We need to be very, very vigilant regarding the low astral planes. We have to be able to use our discernment just as we do here on Earth, and we must always, always have a truly sacred attitude.

The night after the funeral service, Aunt Janine came to visit me in a dream. *She was in the form of energy that came and went in my body. I saw her as blue and mauve energy, coming and going through my body. She was fascinated by my energy, by my level of spiritual conscience, and by the fact that I was the only one able to communicate with her in the funeral home. She was like a little girl, playful and delighted with her new existence. She spoke to me with deep, heartfelt tenderness, saying, "No one believes or understands who you are. It's so amazing, so great what you are, what you are becoming, what you will become."* I was very happy to have encountered her because each concrete proof strengthened and reinforced me in a society that didn't endorse the Metaphysical Worlds. Yet, they are so real!

54. Jean's Car

My brother-in-law, Jean, is a true brother for me. He is a lawyer and a great philanthropist, as well as co-founder, along with myself and my wife, of the non-profit association Universe/City Mikaël. We live in wonderful harmony, we are on the same wavelength, and we share a marvelous bond of friendship and trust. All these years, he has been at our side, giving us all his support and helping us expand our Angelic Mission on Earth. I'll tell you in a later chapter how we met and you'll see how Destiny, with a capital D, truly orchestrated our encounter and alliance on Earth in order to help make the Angels known. (*cf.* Chapter 9 : 65 The Telephone Book)

One day he and his family went to the funfair on St-Helen's Island near the city of Montreal. His car was stolen from the car park there and then found again a few days later. Two months after this theft, Jean told me about an experience he'd just had. He told me that he had intuitively felt that his car was going to be stolen again, so returned to the supermarket car park to check. As he'd had a first career in the police force, this was very unusual for him; he wasn't at all the sort to cultivate fears. Then I told him the dream I'd received the previous night. *I was in a car park and I saw two young thieves about to steal Jean's car. I quickly went over toward them saying, "No, no, no, you're not to steal Jean's car. He had it stolen two months ago, so that's enough. Off you go, guys." And I saw Jean in the distance walking toward his car.* Jean smiled at me and thanked me with all his heart. As he was used to hearing me talk about premonitory information, and since he was used to receiving premonitions himself or through his wife, he knew that this angelic work had really and truly taken place. Working with the Angels has made us all a very special family at the UCM foundation, and I am no longer alone, that's for sure.

55. The Seventh Sign

The last concert I gave before completely retiring from the music world, was for the United Nations, for the Canadian armed forces' peace-keeping mission from 1993-1996. I had accepted to go to the army base in Haiti to participate in the annual show for the soldiers on mission in that country. During that same period, I had been very moved and inspired by a film starring Demi Moore, entitled *The Seventh Sign*, which starts in Haiti. The film is actually a little too intense, too apocalyptic, but at that time, my life was in complete upheaval. The Initiatic Seals had been opened, and the earthquakes and volcanoes of my inner world were fully active. Normally I wouldn't have accepted this last concert, especially as it was co-produced by my daughter's mother, and we had only just separated; the wounds in our heart were still very present. However, because it was in Haiti, and since I wanted to encourage the peace-keeping forces as well as help the local population, I accepted the invitation. The night before my departure, in a dream, *I met a high-ranking officer in the Canadian army. He was there in the dream and he told me that we were to meet, that we had a mission to accomplish together.* The following day, we were to be flown out to the United Nations base in Haiti in a military plane. I saw him the minute I arrived at the first meeting before we took the army bus that was to bring us to the military airport. He was the officer in charge of security, the very same officer as in my dream. He was also a martial arts instructor and he emanated beautiful wisdom. Divine Magic once again! He was identical to the man in my dream, although I had never laid eyes on him in my life. As soon as we got onto the bus to go to the military airport, our eyes met and our souls recognized each other. We spent the whole trip in each other's company and, just the two of us, we did long meditations in several sites and churches in that country. At that time, it was forbidden for civilians to travel anywhere in the country without a military escort. However, beyond military duty, he and I had an encounter with destiny. He became one of the first students with whom I shared angel work and my knowledge regarding the interpretation of dreams, signs, and symbols. He later became a key person in helping us lay the very first stones of our future angelic foundation.

Thus, in dreams, I met the key people who have become the pillars of our Initiatic School, Universe/City Mikaël. And I continue to meet important future contacts in my dreams. For me, each encounter is a mystical story in itself. I could tell you so many mystical encounters like this. When we activate our angelic consciousness, life becomes a true blessing every single day.

CHAPTER SEVEN
ON THE WINGS OF LOVE

In this chapter, Kaya rediscovers love after believing that he'd have to spend the rest of his life alone, serving God and the Angels. He shares with us the dreams he received announcing that Christiane would be his wife. He openly shares how, with her, he re-learned how to love, how to incarnate the masculine and the feminine, how to live as a couple. He deepens his Knowledge with his wife Christiane and their children – his daughter Kasara, and her son Jean-Pierre. Together they develop and learn to become involved on a humanitarian level, hence becoming an angelic family. With them, Kaya moves on to further stages of evolution and the incarnation of angelic energy on Earth and in the Parallel Worlds.

56. The Heart has Reasons that Reason Ignores

Quite frankly, I had de-programmed the idea of ever again having a woman in my life because all that was important for me was to serve Heaven on Earth. God kept well hidden from me the gift He was preparing. Today, I thank Him with all my heart and soul because love with a woman had always been complicated for me. I had become a kind of angelic monk and that suited me fine. I could easily have remained so for the rest of my life on Earth.

After my separation from my daughter's mother, I had a serious relationship with another woman, but it quickly ended after I received a dream *telling me that if I stayed with her, I would have a difficult future.* Feeling deep fear, I left her the very next day, promising myself never to hurt anyone ever again. Even though that woman had betrayed me, I had forgiven her, and continued the relationship sincerely believing that, in my dreams as well as in concrete reality, I could help her transform and re-program herself divinely. Nothing anyone did to me was ever seriously wrong for me. I always found it easy to forgive, and I always gave the other person a chance to renew themselves. Several people in my affective, or professional life had betrayed me in various ways but I wasn't in the least put out or resentful in any way. Like a high level diplomat, I arranged everything so that there was never any conflict. I loved evolution with all my heart and soul, and I believed that everything could be repaired. I wholeheartedly believe this to be true, and I continue to live like this today, except that today I no longer try to do the work for others.

This one serious relationship after my separation was based on my wanting to be a savior. When we met, her boyfriend had just committed suicide, and he had come to see her in a dream to encourage her to commit suicide too. Physically, she was a very beautiful woman. However, she had serious drug and alcohol problems. I had met her at an A.A. (Alcoholics Anonymous) meeting. Those meetings had become my new church even though I had never had any drug or alcohol problems in my life. I used to find myself talking to her in dreams, and, in dreams as well as in reality, I was always concretely helping her to stay alive, not to commit suicide and go and join her former boyfriend. This relationship taught me a lot, and after it my life as a hermit was activated and lasted several years before I met the woman who would become my wife.

57. She will be Your Wife

After this last relationship, living alone without any affective relationship for several years allowed me to activate the great transformation that I went through. But we don't have to be alone to become angelic and live angelically. Today, I am convinced that when we have met the right person, when we have met our true twin soul, we can activate and discover the highest levels of love and mystical fusion as a couple. At that moment there can be an encounter of God's two polarities, the masculine and the feminine. Living with an angelic woman is truly extraordinary because a woman expresses divine powers differently from a man, and this complementarity creates unique, sublime harmony and wonderful, angelic synergy.

However, before such a cosmic encounter could materialize in my life, I had to go through a deep affective weaning stage that allowed me to cleanse my memories of needing to love and be loved. Firstly, I, who had always done my best to ensure everyone was happy, found myself having to learn to say Yes and No in the right way, to love myself, and to get to know myself in great depth. This intense period was part of the angelic teachings I received in dreams, and more often than not, in nightmares.

Emotional memories are actually the most difficult parts of the process of conversion from an ordinary conscience to a universal, unconditional, angelic conscience. We often talk of unconditional love, and we could easily think it is a kind of abstract love, with no real involvement, complications, or deep fusion. *Unconditional* refers to a principle whereby needs have been purified and we have been led to a total acceptance of the Divine Plan and its manifestation in any form. In fact, to act divinely, it is essential to have integrated the concept of not needing anything in return, which doesn't mean we never receive anything. Quite the contrary is true. The more unconditional our love is, the more we love everyone, and this is how we integrate an understanding of the Laws governing the different *sectors* or *departments* of love. Love for our friend, mother, father, brother, sister, neighbor, etc. doesn't manifest in the same way, and yet it is all love.

People very often tend to think that on the spiritual, emotional and affective levels there are no rules or regulations, that there are no Laws to be obeyed, but the opposite is true. The more we evolve divinely, the more precise Laws and rigorous rules there are to be respected. However, since we usually respect them, naturally we don't feel them. It's as if there weren't any. We don't feel restricted in any way. Just as when we reduce speed and drive slowly in a neighborhood where children are playing, we don't feel restricted by an imposed speed limit; our right intention unconsciously, automatically, helps us respect the law.

It is very important to understand the concept of Divine Laws and Structures. The Universe, God, is a set of pre-established Laws and Rules that we have to discover and integrate. They are essentially based on the application of all the Divine Qualities, Virtues and Powers. That's why, in an angelic conscience, we continually refer to this essential aspect of developing Qualities and Divine Powers. *Divine* means that they are right and just, that they respect the Laws of Creation and Cosmic harmony. These Laws are interconnected. Unconditional love is no longer unconditional and right if we are unfaithful, if we desire and envy someone else's life, etc. It is the fusion of numerous qualities that creates true purity. One day, we attain bliss and plenitude because we respect the Laws of Love and Wisdom. That is what true Happiness, what true, happy Longevity is. It's the same for a society where there is no war. Peace provides an opportunity for expansion and abundance to prosper and last.

To attain such a high level of happiness, we have to develop absolute trust in Divine Justice, in the fact that we always receive what is good for our own and others' evolution. If we are alone and haven't yet encountered love, it's because that is the right path for us at the moment. I met my angelic wife, Christiane, at a time when I had absolutely no need for anyone in my life. I had become so content and felt so good living alone; I had succeeded in completely transforming my needs for love to be happy. A ray of sunshine caressing my skin, the fragrance of a flower, a child's smile, even seeing other people happy, in love, made me happy, without needing to experience love physically, because, according to my life plan, it simply wasn't time for me to do so. I totally and completely accepted this fact and I would never have wanted a person in my life who hadn't first been authorized and confirmed by Up Above in a dream. Hence, I was able to become deeply happy while alone. I was able to discover other facets of love that I wouldn't have seen or understood if I hadn't been alone and gone through this affective weaning period. Later, I attained Enlightenment in my heart and my emotional memories after a long journey or voyage, where the first stage was to discover myself, understand self-love as well as love for God in all Creation, to then be able to manifest it with a woman.

In my work to transform and transcend distorted, impure love, you can't imagine just how many nightmares I had. My work to transcend sexuality was so, so difficult at the beginning. Sometimes, I had to close my eyes when I saw a woman in the street so difficult was it not to have had any sexual relationship for months. Of course, it wasn't always like this since my initiations varied according to the subjects my conscience was working on and purifying. Sometimes, however, the days when my emotional needs were activated, I could feel the animal, instinctual part in me and at the mere sight of a woman, I could feel all the pheromones circulating around her. Even as far away as 300 feet, I knew, I could sense if a woman had affective, emotional needs. It was so powerful that temptation was very strong. With a single glance, I could gauge whether I could seduce the woman or not.

Angelic experimentations that allow us to develop our clairsentience are very, very difficult to go through at first. Angelic powers are real and very powerful. Everything in us expands: perceptions, odors, untranscended needs. I think that *Twilight,* the new film and TV series featuring vegetarian vampires is very interesting because such films are a good metaphysical, symbolic explanation of what happens within us when we are studying and striving to develop our angelic nature. Over time, everything within us becomes stabilized and is purified, and we feel relieved and lighter. While maintaining activated extra-sensorial perceptions, we no longer feel such thirst, such lacks, such an extreme need to nourish ourselves affectively and sexually through others, which can sometimes lead to obsession. Initiations to become an angel are very real, I can assure you. I know every stage by heart. My duty today is to teach them so as to facilitate the process of integration for you, because the more you invoke one of the 72 Angels, the more you enter into and activate your power of conscience.

The first time I was told in a dream that Christiane was to be my wife, I didn't believe it at all. I just thought that Up Above was testing me once again. I was absolutely convinced that I would be alone for the rest of my life, because I thought that my degree of knowledge had become too high for me to be in a couple. Following parameters that we normally associate with the religious life of priests, monks, etc., being alone had become a sacrifice I felt was necessary to be free to serve Humanity on Earth. Today, I understand that a person cannot be fully accomplished on the spiritual level if he hasn't learned to live in a couple. Being alone is a beautiful, very important, noble stage if it is lived spiritually, respecting Divine Laws, but it is only a stage in our development. It is not the final stage as we might believe, or be led to believe by certain monastic or religious communities. Many religious orders secretly teach their members that being in a couple, having children, etc., is a karmic life, a life where the person hasn't understood that only God is important, and all the rest is mere distraction for his mind, spirit, and development.

Today, after many years of angelic marriage, of dreams and teachings received from the Parallel Worlds, I know, beyond all doubt, that we have to re-integrate our creative powers, not only to construct nirvana on the inside, but also on the outside. I also understand why the symbol of the Dalaï Lama came to tell me in a dream that I had no business being with them, that I had to move on and prepare a new stage of conscience for Humanity, an Angelic stage of spiritual integration and the marriage of spirit and matter.

Divine love between a man and a woman is a force that leads to multi-dimensional well-being, both on Earth and in dreams. It establishes exceptional, creative, productive capacities in the couple. Encountering our twin soul is so powerful! And I can assure you that it is the gift God offers, and will offer, to all those who work intensely with the Angels. Not only do I see it with Christiane and myself, but also with the numerous couples that have formed while working with the 72 Angels, and received the identity, or confirmation of the identity, of their twin soul in a dream.

58. The Woman of Experience

When we meet our twin soul, we realize that our entire life was prepared and formatted so that this encounter could take place. My wife is Swiss and during my teenage studies, every time I was asked to do a presentation of a country, I always chose Switzerland. I had no idea why. No one in my family had visited Switzerland; none of my friends or neighbors came from there; my choice seemed to be totally unfounded. And that's just a tiny, minor example of a sign compared to another sign I received that has become one of the most beautiful inspiring legends for all of French-speaking Canada. My meeting Christiane was written in a premonitory song, one of my greatest hits that long remained number 1 in the radio charts. Even today, this song is played on the radio every day, and it has become a conscious or unconscious spiritual sign for millions of people.

I was in my twenties, working on my 5th album with Sony Music Canada. Celine Dion had just released a very successful album in French with the top French-speaking composer, Luc Plamondon. I had worked with Luc at the age of 10 when I starred in the rock opera, *Starmania*, one of the most successful musicals in the French-speaking world from the 70s to the 90s. Since my management team had worked on this project with Luc, Vito

asked him if he could possibly write a song for my new album. And having worked so closely with me for all those years of my childhood, he agreed. Luc was responsible for my turning professional at the age of 9 when I was chosen for the musical, which was performed for years.

With my friend and colleague, Marc Provençal, I had composed a very inspiring melody that was destined for great success, and Luc Plamondon wrote the lyrics. While recording and composing this album, entitled *When You Give Yourself (Quand on se donne)*, I had jotted down a pseudo text about humanitarian aid, and the possibility of helping Africa to the sound of the beautiful melody. I was sure that Luc would come up with similar lyrics. I will never forget receiving the fax with his text. As I write this book, I can see it in my mind's eye as clearly as if it were only yesterday. I felt so honored and moved to be working with Luc again. He was, and still is, one of the greatest French-speaking songwriters of our time. So there I was fervently reading the text line by line as it came through on the fax machine. When I came to the title, *A Woman of Experience*, I was so disappointed.

The song speaks about a young man who meets an older woman and who experiences angelic love with her, a sixth sense connection, and so on. But I felt very discouraged because that text seemed so unlike me; I couldn't identify with it at all at the time. I remember calling Vito, my manager, and openly sharing my disappointment. However, we agreed to keep it as it was because Luc wouldn't compose other lyrics for me. I felt so sad and discouraged to have to sing it, little knowing that this song was actually premonitory, and even described my future relationship in every detail. It even mentions the exact age difference between myself and Christiane. It described what our encounter would become and did become years later.

What's more, at that time, I didn't like love songs and every time I sang one, I always sang it for God because I wasn't capable of singing one truly for a woman. It was really special what I felt, believed, and experienced regarding love. For me, love was a great concept that was unattainable on the human level. Of course, in my affective life, I had experienced wonderful moments of love, but deep down, I very often felt flaws in my relationships. With my eternal perfectionism, I always managed to be disappointed or unfulfilled on the intimate level. And having an easily accepting nature, I had come to the conclusion that it was like this for everyone.

I also wrote songs that today seem so insignificant and ordinary to me. I was 16 or 17 years old when I started composing and I was never 100% satisfied with what I wrote. I felt as though there was a wall in my head, an inaccessible place, as though a limitation had been implanted in my brain to function in such and such a way. I long questioned that feeling I had, that wall, that limitation, which caused me to follow passing trends and compose songs that were commercial hits but weren't worth much in my eyes. Very few of my past songs are worth anything today, even if each of them holds a key or code to what I was and what I was going to become, which can be analyzed and understood today. (This is true of all of our experiences; they all tell us something about ourselves, who we were, what we sought, what we needed to work on.) But, *A Woman of Experience* is and always will be a beautiful song, a slice of destiny. And I thank Luc Plamondon with all my heart and soul for having received his inspiration from the Superior Worlds. This song also served as guidance, one of the most beautiful confirmations I've ever received regarding my future life.

Several years later the song became reality, its premonition came true, but you can imagine how difficult it was for me when I began receiving dreams telling me Christiane was going to be my initiate wife, my gift from God. Christiane had been my best friend, my confidante, my heart and soul sister, for several years, how could she become my wife? I loved her *too much* for that; it wasn't necessary to live as a couple, that was my reflection and conclusion. But like a good, wise, loving parent, Up Above continually veils stages from us when we aren't ready for them, or would act and decide differently, and hence thwart our life plan. We are not robots because we gradually learn what we are capable of integrating, while simultaneously having collective pre-programmed stages that inter-connect with other people's destinies. Consequently, certain broad lines have to be synchronized at very precise moments. Of course, a plan can always be changed. We may be replaced, and there are always *back-ups* to take over if we aren't right, if we don't act correctly, or if we become delayed in our life-program. The train can always be re-directed if we over-resist. However, most of the time, the possibility of receiving and knowing our life plan in advance only manifests when we are well advanced on the spiritual level. Generally speaking, it is veiled from us to protect us just as children are not ready for detailed knowledge of life and its consequences. Yes indeed, even though I had a lot of premonitory dreams, I also had my share of surprises; meeting Christiane was one of the most beautiful. I wouldn't have been ready to meet her earlier. Her arrival in my life was perfectly timed to help me through another stage of my angelic journey.

59. The Wedding Dream

Christiane and I met and re-discovered each other in this life, as children might have done. Our relationship began in friendship, in the innocence and purity of a relationship of mutual affection. The very first time we met, it was as if I had always known her. Our relationship was so natural, and Christiane's goodness, kindness, *joie de vivre*, grace, the sparkle in her eye, her love of God, her eternal youth touched the very depths of my soul. I shared my deepest initiations with her, feeling a real sense of true fusion, since she too was going through similar experiences, as a woman. For her first lecture on the Angels, she presented the Angelic State of Conscience 70 Jabamiah, and the theme was: Accompanying the Dying. For this first lecture, without telling her, I bought a whole advertising page in the regional newspaper, and she gave her first public sharing in Canada to a full house. I was so convinced by what she had shared with me about her research and discoveries, that after only 2-3 weeks of Angel work, it was perfectly natural for me to make this philanthropic gesture. I was on Earth to make Angel Teaching known. My life had been prepared for this since I was born. I loved, and still love, the philanthropic aspect of being in the background, and seeing the fruits of helping people

discover the true meaning of an Angel. Serving Heaven is such a wonderful state of grace and such a powerful feeling. When we realize that having a Mission gives such greater meaning to our life than just eating, sleeping, working, and going about our various responsibilities, it is simply extraordinary to live this concretely every day. There are now several great philanthropists who help our foundation. And today I enjoy being with them, making plans, and deciding on projects, as much as that first occasion when I bought the advertising page in the newspaper.

I don't need to tell you that Christiane was very surprised, and the day she was to give her first lecture, it was so intense for her, there was a real mini earthquake in the town where we lived. For her too, sharing in public gave rise to all sorts of memories where, in other lives, people had been very intense toward her. Now knowing our past lives, we know that one of the things we have in common are several past lives of spiritual Mission. We are well aware of the fact that what we have accomplished today began and was in preparation for a very long time.

After that first lecture, and several weeks of sharing, I retreated into more and more solitude to deepen my research and work with Angelic Forces and Powers. And Christiane always came to the rescue when the warrior of light that I was in the process of becoming felt momentarily exhausted and discouraged. We would phone each other to share and, with all her goodness and love, my trustworthy friend, sister, confidante, was always there to help, comfort and inspire me to continue the work I was doing on my deepest personal and collective memories. She too was going through powerful initiations while invoking the Angels, and being able to share and talk about these experiences with one another created a magical, inexplicable link. For a long time, the Happiness, the Love that was right next to me, what Christiane was going to become for me was kept veiled. I was evolving, opening my conscience, and gaining access to Knowledge, but, at the same time, part of me was unconsciously becoming rigid, extremist and too solitary. I often tell my hermit friends that being a hermit is not the be all and end all of evolution, as we might tend to believe while we forge our conscience with our new knowledge. It is a stage that can even be dangerous. The hermit stage does indeed comprise intense, worthy work on ourselves, but it is not the end of the line, so to speak. We can create spiritual haloes and auras, refuges, and even hair shirts to strengthen and reinforce ourselves on the hard, rocky path of our spiritual journey, but later, we will have to de-program them all. Illusion is educational, and it takes a long time before we no longer need it. When the divine love of a couple is revealed to us, we revise all that we have learned about life, and our spouse becomes the manifestation of our inner world, our living mirror.

At the time everything was revealed to us, I received dreams announcing that Christiane was to be my wife first; Christiane received them later. After these troubling revelations, I distanced myself for a while because I didn't want to spoil or harm in any way the sacred friendship, the exceptional, spiritual relationship that we had. After several months of work on myself, I recontacted Christiane, and she suggested that we could work together teaching our angelic experience. I could see our relationship advance and I still had those dreams in mind, but, with discipline and rigor, I put them aside and told myself we could work together to serve Heaven as spiritual friends. Maybe my dreams actually meant just that: a metaphysical union, not a physical one. This concept suited me fine; my rational mind was happy and satisfied with that idea. Consequently, I was able to work in symbiosis with her and maintain our multi-dimensional connection. By that time, after months and months of work with Angel 20 Pahaliah, I had completely transcended my sexuality so I was completely at ease with the idea of a close spiritual friendship, and there was no disturbing dormant desire within me at all.

A couple – a man, who had done very well in the construction business, and his wife, who were friends of ours – attended our very first Angel lectures, and wished to help us build our Mission. They invited us to come and visit some land that could serve as a construction site for Universe/City Mikaël. I will remember that day as long as I live. Christiane and I sat next to each other in the back seat. It was the first time we had sat so close to one another. The journey lasted a good 2 hours. For the first time I began to feel physically attracted to Christiane. I didn't understand my feeling at all because I perceived that it didn't stem from me, but essentially from her, from her energy. I was really perplexed and I speeded up the Angel Mantra Recitation I was doing to erase all trace of this energy, still doubtful whether it was emanating from me or from her. At that time, I had developed the deeply engrained habit of always referring back to myself to cleanse my memories above all else, and because of that, I doubted the very real perceptions I felt seated next to her. I glanced at her out of the corner of my eye, wondering if I would be able to see anything, but, in typical Swiss fashion, Christiane was discretion itself ☺. So, there was nothing visible, no soft, sweet look, nothing at all. It was only what I felt through clairsentience. It wasn't just a light, vague, hazy feeling. It was as though I had been plugged into a city power station, I felt such a strong charge of love activate my heart and body's desire. I was hot and in a real hurry to arrive at our destination to be able to get out of the car. I so wanted to be right and pure with her. My love was greater and more than human in her presence, and that was sacred for me. We arrived and visited the location that could have been a magnificent site for our School, Universe/City Mikaël, but that didn't materialize at the time. After our visit, on the way home, the energy was calmer, there was more well-being and joy simply being together. Nevertheless, something had been activated and things weren't quite the same between us.

Today, we laugh heartily about ourselves; we were so innocent to think that we could work together for the Angels without being married and living our love concretely. We were like a rather uptight priest and nun. Our complete love was veiled from us until the very last minute, until we were ready, in fact. We both had such strong principles and desire to serve the Angels that we could have de-railed Up Above's Plans if we had known them before we were ready. They know what They are doing *Up Above*, I can assure you.

The day after our site visit, the phone rang. Christiane is a direct person and she was calling me to share what she had felt the previous day so as to bring things into the open and set them straight. She told me that during the night she had received a dream showing *me putting my hand on her thigh, tenderly and lovingly*. I'll always remember the moment of silence between us. I knew that a program had been activated because I had been so respectful, I knew that I hadn't projected any energy of the sort toward her. It was a premonitory dream. I stammered a little, while my brain worked as fast as a highly powered computer, going over the dreams I'd been having about this for months. I'd gone away for a while, created a certain distance, I didn't return her calls straightaway, all to remain focused on my Mission. I knew that she was just as intense and determined as I was to serve Heaven, and that this new information could change everything between us. I took a deep breath and began to open up and tell her about the dreams I'd been receiving for a couple of months, which had completely perturbed me. I shared with her the connection with the song *A Woman of Experience*. She didn't know it since she came from Switzerland and in actual fact, she had never been to a concert in her life or even bought a pop record. I could feel that our hearts were now connected, that they vibrated in unison. We decided we would take 3 days to meditate and we would each ask the Angels whether we should form a couple or not.

3 days later, I phoned her. She answered hesitatingly, "Ye..s...h.. ell..o.." I asked her if she was OK and she explained that she was a little dizzy because she was doing a yoga posture standing on her head. Playfully, I asked her, "Is that a sign?" before laughing wholeheartedly, already knowing her answer. She burst out laughing too, and told me she had worked intensely with Angel 18 Caliel, the Angel that always gives us the truth in important moments. One of the dreams she'd received was of *me opening the door for her onto the Light.*

One of our first amorous dates was by a river on a beautiful autumn day. It was magical and we had our first kiss sitting on the rocks like two young teenagers, discovering each other for the first time, still unsure if mum and dad approve. I had been alone for such a long time that being with a woman initiate created great inner upheaval in my years of monastic work. Simultaneously, we both wanted to be right, to follow God and Up Above with all our hearts, and learn what a spiritual couple was. Since everything had begun with a dream, we now understand that it took time for it to descend from the metaphysical level into our thoughts, our hearts, and our bodies, which was actually the perfect development.

Only two weeks later we were living together under the same roof, and on a beautiful sunny day, we set out on a meditative mountain walk. We were so happy to share these moments and at the same time, we didn't really know how to love each other, how to be together. We had to re-learn everything because what in fact was a spiritual couple? An angelic couple? We had both worked so intensely on our needs and instincts that very little made us very happy. Individually, we were both fulfilled, complete in ourselves, and we both enjoyed a very simple lifestyle, and what was wonderful was that we were never ever bored with one another. We trusted each other too. I didn't have to be extra gallant; Christiane was a complete woman and every gesture of mine had to be true and meaningful. We had even discussed the idea that there might not be any need for sexuality in our couple. Today, of course, we find that funny, because how could we have lived without the fusion of our bodies, without those marvelous moments that we now experience together, which regenerate and vivify us and sanctify our mutual well-being? But back then, the idea of no sexuality was plausible for us and on our mountain walk, we decided that we would meditate on this and ask Up Above what we should do.

In silence, we climbed that mountain, vivified by our elevating walk, which was accompanied all the way by Angel Recitation. A light breeze caressed our faces, and the autumnal sun was reassuring and comforting – a magnificent, perfect moment. At the summit, we both settled to meditate and ask what to do about sexuality, was it really necessary? I closed my eyes and silently, with all my heart and soul, I asked, "Is it right for the evolution of our souls to have sexual relations in our couple?" Instantaneously I was surprised to hear a vibrant voice say, "What a twit you are!" *Twit* is an expression used in Quebec which means *completely ridiculous.* I really heard it say this loud and clear in my head, and I burst out laughing. Christiane looked at me laughing till tears streamed down my face. She told me she had received the same answer in her meditation, and that there was no reason why we shouldn't live our love fully. Asking such a question may seem strange to you, but I assure you, it was quite a step for me. Just imagine, I was virtually a priest; it was as though I was about to break my vow of chastity. Furthermore, I was going to have to re-learn and reactivate something that, to my mind, had caused me so many powerful nightmares before being able to free myself from this natural need. Quite a step indeed! So I asked Christiane if she could be the one to decide. I didn't want to be the one who initiated our first intimate relationship. I so wanted to be sure it was right. We agreed it would be her, and even if it took months and months, I didn't mind. I left it up to her to receive the right timing from Up Above.

Just so you know, at that time, we had already been living together for a few weeks. Everything had gone very quickly on that level; I gave up my apartment and we moved in together as a devoted spiritual couple, joyfully and enthusiastically, delighted at being able to be together and talk and share from morning till night. Well, to my great surprise, our first intimate relationship took place 3 days later. Christiane would say, it took 3 days for the idea to be embodied on the 3 levels: head-heart-body. She approached me in a surge of such magnificent purity, and we made love as though for the first time since time began, as though our fusion was setting in motion a new life program for us and all Humanity.

I love Christiane with all my heart and with all my soul. What we live together surpasses everything I could ever have imagined possible in a relationship between a man and a woman.

60. Return to the Source

My ascension toward Angelic Enlightenment resumed and increased in intensity, even while I was with my beloved. However, everything was different; now I had my wife, a gift from God, and now I could have her by my side to help heal my night wounds.

One night, in a dream, *I found myself in an Asiatic prison. I was crouched down on the ground, making myself as small as possible, surrounded by incredible violence. I saw scenes of such violent decadence that I needn't describe them in words. In the dream, I was told that I had been there for 3 years.* When I woke up at 3.30am, I was paralyzed and couldn't walk. My legs were curled up under me in great pain. Christiane woke up to help me by gently massaging my legs. My dream lasted no more than 5 or 6 minutes and yet I felt as though I hadn't walked for 3 years. The pain and paralysis lasted the rest of the night, and only after 3 or 4 hours was I finally able to walk properly again. I was so happy to have Christiane at my side. We had both surpassed our fears of initiations. She knew I was visiting collective forces, that I was continually strengthening and reinforcing my soul to develop the qualities of the greatest initiates so that I would be able to work in the Parallel Worlds and hence become a guide for others, and help souls find their way into the next dimensions. Her presence was a constant source of joy in my heart that I had been a little too strict with, for such a long time. With Christiane, I was learning anew and discovering how to live in a couple, which was overwhelming and awe-inspiring at first.

I remember one of our first evenings together and I was watching and intensely listening to a TV program and analyzing it. Christiane started to prepare supper, so turning off the TV, I immediately got up to help her. Very kindly and forthrightly, she said to me, "It's OK, you can continue to watch and study whatever it is you are watching. I'm fine getting supper for the two of us. For me it is both relaxation and meditation since I always invoke an Angel while I'm doing it. I don't need any help at the moment." I insisted on helping her, used to functioning like this, and she continued to reassure me, saying, maybe another time, but right then, I had to get used to receiving unconditionally, to being helped without instantly wanting to help in return. Oof! I was completely shaken by her words and tears sprang into my eyes and gently rolled down my cheeks. I wasn't used to living like that with a woman. Being as sensitive as a flower, I had always compensated when my preceding girlfriends did anything for me. I sensed and tuned in to their need for us to do things together at the same time. Otherwise, I sometimes received a hail of energy bullets. I told her my deepest thoughts regarding this, and she explained that if I had been doing something too ordinary, she wouldn't have encouraged me to continue. She would have preferred me to participate and be positively active rather than idle my time away. However, she knew that I was listening to the news and that I received dreams about these events, and she'd sensed that my energy was right. That's all that counted in her eyes, not what I was doing. I was very moved by her deep understanding.

Every day, with Christiane, I discovered a new – or renewed – way of living, that I had never experienced in this life. Deep down, however, I already knew all this. It was as though Christiane was re-activating the right way to live. As she gradually taught and accompanied me, I slowly but surely reactivated that distant, former knowledge of the complementarity of a couple in action. At all times, I kept in mind that I had to be right to deserve her love and trust. Hence Christiane helped activate and re-blossom in me what had been deep within me since time immemorial.

Unlike love relationships that fade as time passes, our love continued to grow and expand so much that I often asked myself if it could possibly grow any more, whether there could be another stage. And with time, I learned that the answer was yes; our love continues to deepen and expand beyond all dreams and expectations. Later, when our collective responsibilities had grown and we had hundreds and thousands of students throughout the world, when my dreams telling me that our books would be read by people all over the world had come true, we continued, and continue, to learn together, to function and devote ourselves in a healthy, holy way to this collective, multiplying, associative life. These very brief examples of our love path are a tiny testimonial to the wonderful grandeur of our relationship and fusion on all levels. My wish is that everyone, after long work on themselves, may one day be given the possibility to incarnate Divine Love with their spouse. I didn't believe it was possible on Earth, and with Christiane I've learned that it is. When I take her in my arms and she embodies pure, divine qualities, I very often close my eyes and thank God for allowing me to live this experience, and for being able to renew and replenish myself in her, in the perpetual oasis of her love.

Once again, we had to revise our beliefs. We had thought that our love was so elevated and pure that we didn't need to get married. Today, we know that the contrary is true. We realize that this commitment before God and other people is a sacred act of great trust and confidence. When we receive right, precise dreams and clear signs, we can enter this communion in all sincerity, and hence activate another deeper stage of love. Things went very quickly for us once we'd met and fused. Shortly afterwards, one night in a dream, I found myself *with two white-haired, spiritual elders, who, at the time, symbolically represented patriarchy, wisdom, fidelity to their spouse and to Divine Principles, as well as affective, emotional, and material stability. In my dream, I saw Ken Appleman and Normand Désourdy. They were beautifully luminous, standing side by side. With a loving, serene smile, Ken asked me, "Do you love Christiane?" With all my heart, I said that I did. Then, he looked at me really solemnly and said, "Well then, marry her!"*

The following morning, I asked Christiane if she would like to come for a walk with me. We often used to go for a walk around the village where we lived at that time, St-Sauveur-des-Monts, and we'd either talk and share or simply meditate. Off we went and I remained silent most of the walk, knowing that what I was going to ask her would lead us into another new stage of life. Heaven was setting the pace since we were guided by dreams confirming what was right. When we reached the church, I asked her to sit down on the steps for a moment. I took a few steps away to take a deep breath and then coming toward her, looking deep into her angelic eyes, I asked her with all my heart, "Do you want to marry me?" She looked at me, unsurprised, and with her eyes full of Light, love and devotion, she spontaneously said, "Yes, I do." I encircled her hands with simple wooden rosary beads and took her tenderly into my arms.

Sharing these marvelous, inspiring memories with you, brings to mind another sacred moment that occurred when we were meditating in the mountains one day. At that time, we gave our lectures in the same place where we were later married; it was called *St-Francis-of-the-Birds*. Just before choosing where we would be married, we were praying in the countryside when a bird landed on my hand, and at the very same time, another landed on Christiane's. These signs confirming our fusion, confirming that Up Above approved of our union were so important for us, and confirmed the most beautiful moments of our life. Thus, with Heaven's approval, we were able to discover together the depths of true love, of Angelic fusion in love.

61. Masculine and Feminine

I really understand monks and nuns, or any religious/spiritual people who remain alone. Having chosen never to marry, they don't know what they are missing. Some of them sincerely believe that they have achieved perfect fusion of the masculine and feminine principles within themselves. However, as long as we haven't concretely lived this on the outside, we can only have partial knowledge of such fusion. In a couple, everything is accelerated. We leave our personal comfort and habits behind and experiment a whole new stage of life on all levels. When we are in a couple, it is amazing how life helps us evolve. Of course, when we are spiritual, an ordinary, down-to-earth, non-spiritual relationship is not interesting. It is better to live alone than to be in a complicated, over-materialistic relationship, with power games, jealousy, aggression, attraction and repulsion, etc.

I was much more feminine than masculine, which is actually one of the main characteristics of spiritual men because they are hypersensitive and, more often than not, too soft, too gentle, etc. *Too much* of anything always engenders difficulties and creates imbalance in our way of being and functioning. Whenever we are too soft, others take advantage of us, abuse us, make us feel inferior, and contribute toward the development of an inferiority complex. We are too easily influenced and make poor decisions especially when there is a lot of tension or problems to be solved. We tend not to be rigorous enough because we want to please everyone and because we need to feel loved. Re-polarization is quite a task! And it can only be fully undertaken and experienced in a spiritual, evolutive couple, that continually adjusts until the qualities attained radiate and create balance and well-being in both the woman and the man.

Before meeting Christiane, I attracted more emissive, more masculine, stimulating, controlling, superwoman types. Needless to say, the Law of resonance was putting me in contact with what I lacked on the inside because at that time, I was not rigorous or active, or decisive, or responsible enough, so this kind of woman allowed me to see what I lacked. The other person is

152

like a mirror for us, he or she is always a complementary facet of who we are. Women and men are so different and yet so complementary once they have rediscovered and balanced their respective essences. It is absolutely fascinating how happy we become when right equilibrium and balance is manifested in the couple. Transformation leads to an expansion of our forces and capacities. This is just as true for a woman as for a man. Even our senses begin to work in harmony and complementarity.

Work on the masculine and feminine within ourselves and on the outside is part of a long journey. It's not because we are a spiritual couple that there are no discussions, adjustments, and confrontations. On the contrary, in the beginning, re-polarizing requires tremendous work. It takes hundreds of discussions and situations to learn how to function in total, mutual trust. Mutual attunement is a very fine, complex line to discover. It is just as difficult for a man as for a woman to re-polarize, and when we are an angelic couple, our inner work is both intense and fantastic.

In our case, what was wonderful was that we both had periods of working alone to carry out deep work on our ego and instinctual, basic needs. It is more difficult when this work is done simultaneously in a couple, when both begin their spiritual path together. It is possible, of course; we don't need to be alone to begin an angelic path. In fact, if we are two, it's even better. We just need to have a lot of humility regarding our spouse and know and say the magic words: *I'm sorry*. What's more, we must never take the other's presence and qualities – kindness, gentleness, patience, tolerance, devotion, etc. – for granted. Some people unconsciously seek problems to stimulate their love. When everything is going well, they feel bored. Human nature is really very special sometimes. That's why we need to transcend it and activate our angelic nature, which provides our relationship with a whole other dimension. Not only does our spouse become our lover, but also our friend, our confidante, our father or mother, or work colleague, at times, as well as always being both a teacher and our best school-friend, and possibly fulfilling many other roles too. One day, we re-discover such fusion in the complementarity of an angelic couple that we embody numerous beneficial aspects of our polarity; not only the passionate, lover dimension between

a man and a woman. Consequently we can create beautiful works: children who grow up well-balanced, with true, right, shared values, and all sorts of major and minor projects, founded on and continually inspired by right, true, altruistic intentions.

Ideally men and women shouldn't have quarrels and disagreements; normally, they should always agree. Common sense as to what is right is based on Divine Qualities. When we can't apply qualities, it's because the decision or way we live lacks balance. Of course, life isn't just black and white. There is a whole palette of colors to discover and develop the flexibility to evolve by following what is right. There are conscious and unconscious experimentations that have to be experienced and lived to evolve. We can't hold it against our spouse when he follows what he believes to be right. We have to accept that life guides us toward apprentices or learning experiences that we need to go through, and sometimes toward karmas that we need to repair. When it is karmic, we should never say, "Oh! That's his or her karma." In a couple, we are connected, we are fusional, and there is something for us to understand and integrate too. Spiritual living and journeying together is a wonderful path; it is the greatest and most beautiful path.

62. Christiane, Kasara & Jean-Pierre

Our happiness wouldn't have been complete without the presence of our two children, our daughter Kasara, and our adult son Jean-Pierre from Christiane's former marriage. The development of our angelic conscience allowed us to reprogram and repair some concepts of ordinary life that we had integrated as parents. With her son, Christiane was able to become a new mother, fill a different role, because when he was younger, she hadn't access to this Knowledge or her dreams. With Kasara, we were able to transmit Angelic Knowledge of dreams, signs, and symbols to her at a very young age, and to see, at close hand, all the benefits it engenders. Similarly, opening up to the knowledge of his dreams and signs, Jean-Pierre was inspired and able to develop his magnificent potential and become a responsible, honorable man radiating beautiful qualities. With time, our children have become the most beautiful fruits of what we are, and we are deeply happy to see them blossom so well.

It is true that we have become a bit of an extraterrestrial family ☺. Every morning we share our dreams, our travels into the other dimensions. Each of us receives his own information and guidance; hence we all have our spiritual autonomy. Our children could have cast aside or rejected our Angelic path; on the contrary, they help and support us. They can see all of its benefits themselves as they have had, and continue to have, their own proof.

Kasara, who is now 20 years old, has become an exceptional angelic young woman. She has written two books that have become bestsellers in several countries. She wrote the first one when she was 9 years old. It is called *The Spiritual Diary of a Nine-Year-Old Child*. It talks about her angelic childhood, her dreams, and her perception of life. This book is a unique, true testimony that can help teachers, parents and children to reflect on and discover their own potential. It shows what new children can become when they have daily access to angelic knowledge and development. She wrote her second book at the age of 13, *The Spiritual Diary of a Teenager*. Recently, she has recorded meditational CDs of sung mantras with the 72 Angels, started writing her new book, and she has also begun giving lectures in several countries. We truly have a wonderful life of creativity and sharing. Serving the Angels on Earth through our foundation is an honor and a daily duty.

The journey wasn't easy, especially for me in the first years, but today, God has rewarded me with immense, immeasurable happiness.

CHAPTER EIGHT
ENLIGHTENMENT

Even after his wise, loving marriage with Christiane, initiations continue for Kaya and the author plunges us into a world of phenomenal evolution where the human spirit fuses more and more with its angelic nature. He shares the 4 Angelic Enlightenments he received, the aims and goals, reprogramming and change that they engender in him. In easily accessible, understandable language, he reveals to us what the great sages must have experienced during their powerful transformation, and what they're able to accomplish on the metaphysical and physical levels as a result of these new degrees of conscience. The aim of his sharing these secret stages of his mystical life is to teach us that we can all become angels, that we can all incarnate and embody Divine Qualities and Virtues.

63. Initiations Continue

Now my wife and I share the same bed and it is a real joy for me because my intense initiations are over. Before this however, right at the beginning of our love relationship, we lived in a little mountain apartment. There was a mezzanine we could get to *via* a ladder beside the front door. From there, we could go up into the attic, which is where I chose to sleep, instead of sleeping in the bedroom with my beloved wife, Christiane. My nightmares were very intense and I woke up many times during the night. I preferred to sleep up there, knowing it was only temporary, knowing that one day, I would be able to sleep beside my wife every night, as has been the case for many years now. On really hot summer nights, up there under the roof, the temperature could rise to 115 degrees Fahrenheit, but that didn't bother me at all. My soul was heated up that's for sure, as indeed was my physical body too, but when I was young, I didn't really feel the heat or cold; I had to think about it for it to affect or bother me. Today, it's different; I'm now more incarnated in my body. Christiane is still a great help to me, because we've noticed that as a woman she is more terrestrial, more earthly, in the best sense of the word, whereas I am more up in the air. She very easily senses and feels what is close to her, and I, what is further away. It is very special to live as a couple because even our angelic powers are complementary. Christiane even senses my hunger before I do. She always arrives at the right moment. She constantly answers my thoughts. She tunes into and senses atmospheres and ambiances perfectly. And in the car, she is a more than perfect co-pilot. It's truly impressive how, without any fear or nervousness, she can always intervene and supplement my own vigilance when necessary. It is so beautiful! Without her help, there are quite a few car accidents that Heaven would have had to *remote-control* me to avoid ☺.

All this to tell you that when the two principles, masculine and feminine, join together, they form a wonderful angelic team to serve Heaven on Earth, and it is marvelous to live and experience this as a couple. At times I dream and receive some information and Christiane receives the continuity or complementary information, the piece that helps us understand even better, or that lets us know what is currently in progress. Like me, she helps, treats, and heals others in dreams or in concrete reality. Her simple presence can purify an atmosphere, deeply inspire or bring joy, consolation, and renewed taste for life and living. Her love is so powerful that it modifies everyone who comes in contact with her. To experience that, we have to do truly great work on ourselves, and the path is not always easy.

People sometimes wonder what's the point of having so many nightmares and ordeals. Why do we have to suffer so much? Why do we have to go through inner and outer initiations, and all the different stages of Enlightenment to achieve true Wisdom and Angelic Knowledge? What is the aim and goal of all these inner combats and intense struggle that initiations put us through, either in dreams or concrete reality, or both? Why is it so difficult? Why isn't it easier?

I can reply by telling you that the goal of each and every human being is to become a universal being, to integrate our divine, angelic nature. To become universal, we need to know everything that exists, good and evil. We have to activate and develop the Essences, Qualities, and Divine Laws that allow us to understand how the Universe works. The one and only goal of our multiple incarnations, questioning, and experimentation is to develop Qualities, Virtues, and Powers in their purest, most Divine form, and to understand the Laws and respect them at all times, in all circumstances. To learn all this, to succeed in developing all these qualities, we are given numerous lives, many learning cycles, multiple apprenticeships where we make mistakes and poor choices, which are presented to us again later, either in the same or in another form, until we understand and learn to think, feel and act in a right, just, qualitative manner.

This process of experimentation, of the possibility to discover and get to know the different colors or hues and essences of Creation, leads us to develop the different qualitative *departments* gradually, at our own pace. The only way of knowing a quality is by being able to compare it, to know its opposite; hence, we gradually recognize what helps to create good, what produces healthy fruit. With time, we refine our qualities and we understand the nuances between good and evil. There is a very important sentence to remember, to underline and re-read whenever we feel submerged, deeply shaken, and no longer know the point of our spiritual journey: *An evolved soul is a soul that knows evil and voluntarily chooses not to do it.* Our real aim is to know. Knowledge is the reason for everything we experience and experiment. Receiving beautiful dreams and intense nightmares accelerates our experimentation of life. We experience things more rapidly on the metaphysical level , which means we may not need to go through them in concrete reality. That's why nightmares are as important as beautiful dreams. That's how we cleanse our karmas, our memories, the erroneous attitudes and actions we may have recorded in the past, or thoughts we may have recorded in our soul, in our inner computer, during the course of our different lives. I often tell people that I prefer to have intense nightmares and evolve *via* dreams, rather than have to go through a major, concrete ordeal lasting 20 years or more! Of course, if we find ourselves experiencing such an ordeal, it's because we acted in this negative way, time and time again in another life, not only in unhealthy thoughts or feelings and sentiments, but actually behaving in a very harsh or intensely negative way with people in general, or more specifically, our loved ones. Divine Justice is part of the process of our experimentations and is programmed in accordance with the percentages of essences that we have within ourselves, which indicate how we behave, love, or think. We can do as we wish, but automatically, if we choose a minor or major negative tendency, then we activate small or large-scale negativity. The evidence of our personal autonomy, of our choice in life should always be borne in mind as it is fundamental for our understanding of how the Universe works, how Divine Justice is applied. To awaken and enlighten our lives, we need to inscribe in every cell of our being that our positive choices engender good in our life; that we are master of our destiny, of what we become both individually and collectively. One day we no longer behave, love, or think negatively because we know that this creates negativity in and around us.

Knowledge is simply common sense. Wisdom isn't all that mystical. It is quite simply a cycle of good, right choices over a long period, which consequently engenders good in our life. It is the accumulation of little things that eventually leads to great things.

In the beginning, a negative karma is formed and constructed by lacks, needs, tensions, discomforts, prejudice, reluctance, frustration, and desires that accumulate and accumulate until one day a negative action takes shape in our life: we commit an act that we prepared, that we unconsciously, but very gradually validated through all sorts of rebellious, frustrated attitudes. Deep down we know we aren't right when we swim in murky waters. Everyone knows this. When a criminal commits a crime, he too knows he's wrong, that it's not right to commit this negative act, but he can't help it, because long accumulated memories have led him to an obsessive desire to do whatever he did. It's the animal force in us that has to be transcended, the force that doesn't take the universal aspect into enough consideration, because it focuses on minor, most often exclusively personal detail, on immediate needs. An evolved being is a person who makes conscious choices that are right and good for him, and simultaneously are good and right for others too. It is global vision of our actions, feelings and thoughts that leads to greater understanding and spiritual behavior that have a much vaster effect, far beyond the individual, personal level.

In the beginning, however, we are not all angelic, which is absolutely normal. We have to experiment to become it because it is everyone's goal to develop and help evolve the spark of God's Light that we all have within ourselves, which is connected to the entire Universe. The powers we have are deliberately limited by Cosmic Intelligence so that first of all, we learn in small things before we move on to do bigger, greater things. Everyone's goal is to totally merge and fuse with the Great Whole, to return to our Origin. This is called Enlightenment; i.e. the capacity to recognize that God is an Energy that is in everyone and everything.

64. The 4 Stages of Angelic Enlightenment

In the beginning, the stages of Enlightenment occur through numerous initiations, which, first of all, lead us to discover our conscious self, what we have experienced. In the beginning, we are often shaken to the core, upset, and even disgusted with ourselves when we realize we did such and such a thing that was wrong, that hurt such and such a person. It is not easy to bring our behavior to Light, because we are full of illusions and personal laws that cause us to act in an ordinary, selfish, self-centered way. At the beginning of our angelic path toward Enlightenment, one after the other, the revelations that we receive create and multiply the opening of our unconscious, and make us reflect deeply on our life and behavior. We don't necessarily go through a depression or develop fibromyalgia, but deep ill-being on the psychological and physical levels is engendered. This first stage of self-awareness is perceptible. We become more sensitive, more open, which creates very strong extra-sensorial and cellular perceptions. Consequently we seek to eat better, to improve our environment. We are more easily disturbed by people, smells, sounds, etc. A process of purification is set in motion and may sometimes become extreme, especially in the beginning, when we may tend to judge ourselves and others, exclude them, and/or want to impose our values, our principles, etc.

This gradual opening of our consciousness and unconscious occurs simultaneously, parallel to self-knowledge. Initiations essentially exist to lead us to understand everything that scares or frightens us. Everything that aggresses us is actually parts or aspects of ourselves, of our unmanifested personality, of our deep unconscious. In the beginning, we have to work on and cleanse our personal memories. First of all, in our dreams, we have to visit who we really are, problems in our close personal sphere. If we learn to analyze others using the Law of resonance, always referring back to ourselves, it very rapidly becomes easier. Working like this, using constant self-referral, becomes an extraordinary source of knowledge that helps us not to judge other people severely, and not to destroy our relationships or the environment in which we live and experiment. With Angel work, we realize that others are parts of ourselves that, most of the time, unwittingly help us evolve.

We cannot understand others if we don't know ourselves. In the development of angelic conscience, it is essential to know this. The ancient proverb *Know yourself and you will know the Universe* defines, in a way, the dynamics of spiritual evolution that lead a person to develop divine powers and capacities. We only know a tiny percentage of what we are and of what we can become. The symbolism of an angel is an ideal image of what disembodiment is, what traveling beyond our terrestrial world is. One day, the activation of spiritual, universal powers becomes the gift that the 4 Enlightenments bestow on our life.

There are 4 Angelic Enlightenments that we can attain. Of course, if we add up the multiple phases and stages, this number could easily be modified. Nevertheless, in work with *The Traditional Study of Angels*, 4 major stages are confirmed to us in dreams to let us know that we have achieved the activation of our divine qualities and angelic spiritual powers.

1. Angelic Enlightenment on the intellectual level
2. Angelic Enlightenment on the emotional level
3. Angelic Enlightenment on the physical level
4. Angelic Enlightenment on the spiritual level

Stage 1: The Arrow

I received my first Angelic Enlightenment during our honeymoon in Miami. A friend had invited us to stay at her apartment while she was away on business. How lucky I was to have an initiate wife because I had so many, many, many intense nightmares that I very often had to go for a walk on my own along the beach in order to liberate tensions and solve the enigmas received in my dreams. Christiane understood and accompanied me in her heart and soul with so much love and wisdom. An ordinary wife could easily have become angry and been disappointed; but not Christiane, not at all. She too received her answers *via* her intuition and dreams, and she knew that what I was going through was right and positive.

During the process of setting the first Enlightenment in motion, everything became all confused in my head. The doses of information to reflect on and classify became almost unbearable. I didn't know my first Enlightenment was underway, and as usual, I remained discreet about what I was going through, even to my wife. I didn't feel like telling her everything I saw since most of it was bleak and horrific. I did wonder if something was in preparation because my mind was almost overwhelmed with the sheer intensity of what I was experiencing. Moreover, I knew that it wasn't usual because Up Above had chosen my honeymoon, where I ought to have been in top form to enjoy this happiness with my wife. They are wonderful pedagogues, Up Above; They know where and when to find us to de-stabilize or disturb us if we have the slightest desire for comfort. When I say that military training is nothing in comparison with Angelic training, I know what I'm talking about. My wife, who received her first Enlightenment shortly afterwards, understood and loved me. She had such confidence in me when very often I had none whatsoever for myself.

The night of my first Enlightenment, it was as if a whole country was being bombarded with atomic forces. I was used to these powerful encounters, but this time, what I saw in my dreams was really, really frightening. A psychiatrist, had I consulted one, would probably have had me interned for the rest of my life. Especially when after waking up, I behaved perfectly normally. I was a flawless secret agent, with no aggressive projection onto anyone, and never ever onto my wife. Mastery of negative thoughts is crucial for the first Enlightenment. I learned such mastery through what I experienced, and also alongside some of my students who have overcome this hurdle, and passed this difficult, intense stage.

The dream announcing that I had passed the mystical ordeal was simple and very precise. After being intensely bombarded with nightmares, in series of a minimum of 45 dreams, one after the other, in the same night, just like magic, along came the final, confirming dream, activating perfect calm.

I saw a kind of diagram behind my head, level with my medulla (i.e. at the base of my head, just above the upper end of my spinal cord). I was shown what looked like 3 arrowheads pointing upward as though indicating 3 floors in this region, one above the other. And, physically, in my head, I felt pulses of magnetic energy that opened the final arrowhead (like an A without the bar). The other two were already open. I understood that they were like gates of receptivity and energy circulation, which allowed me to increase the flow of energy to my medulla. I saw myself in a kind of room that was all white, and doctors and guides there were supervising me. I felt a very intense current of electricity. It was as though I could see an X-ray, while simultaneously living this experience in my mind. Once the gate was opened, I was told that I had been adjusted, that my Enlightenment had been attained.

I woke up with such peace and serenity in my mind. Christiane was asleep beside me. I looked up at the ceiling and all around me. I didn't feel like a different person from the previous evening. I was calm, as calm as though a stage had quite simply been completed. I didn't feel like talking about it or announcing it. It was as though, after years of study, I had passed an intense doctorate exam, and I was now quite at peace with what I had accomplished.

Later, in the hours and days that followed, I realized that I understood everything much more easily, that I had no more doubt about the fact that everyone was here on Earth to evolve spiritually. I watched TV, observed people and life all around me, with that absolute certitude in my mind. Today, I realize that first Enlightenment was a solidification of dynamics that have become immutable in my conscience since then. I also realize that, like many people who experience moments of perfect well-being during meditation, I had already experienced this understanding, this mental plenitude and fulfillment with God, but it hadn't been a stable, steadfast, integral part of me. After this Enlightenment, in my mind, and indeed, in all of me, on every level of my being, the concept of God was an absolute fact. Since then, this state has remained stable, solid, steadfast and unwavering within me. The perception and understanding that God is everywhere, that He is Divine Energy in everyone and everything, was the answer to everything, even to what I didn't understand. Now, any questions I may have regarding daily life are only passing enigmas, helping me advance further in my involvement, in my experimentation, and in my discovery on the Divine level.

Stage 2: The Heart

Years later, the second Enlightenment came to me to raise and stabilize my level of unconditional love. The type of initiation related to this stage is emotionally very difficult. I saw my friends and family in dreams; one day they loved me, and the next day, they didn't. I saw people, false promises, short-lived feelings and sentiments, emotional and sexual dependencies, multiple stories of love and hate, friends for a day, and those for life. As we advance toward Enlightenment on the heart or emotional level, what is most difficult is to be shown *the temperature* of people, situations, and events each night in our dreams. Thus, we study true and false grief and sorrow, and we receive intense dreams of tsunamis, cargo ships capsizing, and couples separating. Dreams of rain, rain, and more rain! Dreams where we are insulted, disowned, mocked and scorned. Dreams where we see our own wife leaving us, abandoning us, and we have to remind ourselves that in the dream, she is a symbol, not our real wife, but a symbol embodying memories related to past inner forces. We suffer and we see ourselves in past emotional, affective memories, in the arms of our ex-girlfriends (or ex-boyfriends); we see them suffer, we accompany them. Dreams with seemingly endless emotionally ambivalent, complicated scenarios interspersed with beautiful dreams where ex-partners, all dressed in white, thank us. Once again, it's not concrete reality; they are symbols, and we mustn't ring them up the following day to thank them, because they'd only wonder what on earth was the matter with us. One after another, all sorts of scenario upon scenario lead us to visit and explore the theme of love in all its forms.

We learn to love without any expectations. We help a sick person and he may thank or ignore us, or become too demanding. Then along come other intense dreams where thousands of people, whole races insult and reject us; other scenes where we see them reject their love for God; multiple scenes where they only think of themselves. Some mornings we cry our heart out, imprinted with scenes of such sadness no film could ever portray or express. This is because scenes in dreams are essences of real life, complete egregores (*cf.* footnote p. 89) that are filtered through our emotional body.

A final dream announced my passageway to a new, emotional, affective conscience, to angelic love that erases all painful, past energy, and inscribes in us, in each and every one of our cells, sensitive understanding and infinite love; love that always sees good in deepest evil, in the heart of every ordeal. I will always remember the dream telling me that I had attained Enlightenment on the heart level.

I found myself in the Tree of Life, in the sephirah Netzach, which, in ancient angelic tradition, represents Angelic Love, gentleness, happy solutions, happiness, beauty and esthetics, as well as refinement. Jesus and Buddha were also present. It was as though it was their planet, their home. There were children of all races and nations. A world without war, without violence, in a beautiful, majestic, peaceful landscape. Everything in this place was easy. Rivers, lakes, and seas of incredible beauty that don't exist on Earth. There were also women and men, couples of sublime beauty, radiating indescribable love for God and all of Creation.

Stage 3: The Keys to the Worlds

The third Enlightenment concerns the physical level. It is a cycle of initiations where we obtain access to divine materialization. It allows us to become incorruptible, upright, and honest. It leads us to experience great moral and physical ordeals so that we are no longer ever afraid of losing anything, not even our own life. Each cycle of Enlightenment leads us to re-live the preceding cycles. Hence, the intellectual, emotional, affective levels are worked on more deeply, according to the same principle as learning mathematics at school. When we begin learning, we acquire the basic fundamental principles that allow us to do some equations, but, the more we advance and go on to the next levels, the more complex, precise and specialized the operations become. The apprenticeship cycles of Enlightenment are carried out over several lives. When we reach certification level, Up Above announces it to us in a series of dreams and a final examination, which, in a clearly defined way, confirms the fact that we have indeed integrated one of the levels of Angelic Enlightenment.

Physical-level Enlightenment is specifically concentrated on our capacity to materialize and material detachment, with the aim of transcending our need to succeed, etc. Through this Angelic stage, a person attains a degree of evolution and manifestation where he is in total symbiosis with his environment, projects, and concrete materializations. He no longer needs things or objects to live happily. That doesn't mean that he no longer materializes, quite the contrary. Everything is undertaken with a new conscience and all accomplishments are an integral part of the Divine collective level. Egoism no longer exists; the ego has fused with Divine Will.

A powerful dream confirmed my reaching this important stage in angelic living.

I was dressed in white, and with my two feet firmly on the Earth, I was looking up at Heaven. I felt good, peaceful, calm and serene. There was an atmosphere of loving-kindness, deep benevolence, and the knowledge that henceforth, everything was possible for me on Earth, and at the same time, I didn't need anything. I felt a state of absolute detachment. At one point, a column of Light came down from Heaven. I began to levitate, to rise up and up in the column of pure, bright, white Light. As I rose, I saw objects dance all around me, symbols representing actions, situations I had been through... they appeared and disappeared in an energy of fulfillment, as though all of that was over, finished, terminated; as though I could have everything but I needed nothing. There was the Source of Light above me, and It gently aspirated me up toward It, toward Heaven. I found myself above the symbols, arms stretched out in the shape of the cross, head leaning slightly back looking up toward Heaven. My body was lit up with indescribable Happiness, and I continued to rise upward in the column of Light. At one point, I found myself very close to the Source of Light, that indescribable Force that instilled such peace, such bliss, such beatitude in me. In this blissful state of soul and spirit, in my mind, through telepathy, I heard the question as to whether I wanted to continue and fuse with the Light. I understood that I had the choice of fusing with the Light or returning to help on Earth. My whole body trembled and shook, so powerful was the Light. All my senses were present. It was a feeling of coming Home, an incredible, indefinable feeling where problems didn't exist any more. I knew that if I continued I was going to die and my body would be consumed by the Earth. Still trembling all over, so pure and powerful were the rays of Light flooding my whole body, I looked at the Light, and solemnly declared to the Source, "I willingly accept to serve, to continue my Mission on Earth to help others."

Instantaneously, there was a change of scene, and I found myself in front of a curtain of stars against a black background. It was so real and pure; as if the galaxy, the Universe had been drawn, was reflected on the curtain. A man approached me and asked, "Can you lend me the key you're wearing around your neck?" I asked him, "What do you need it for?" realizing that indeed I did have an indescribably beautiful, gold and crystal key around my neck. Not answering my question, he repeated his request more insistently, like an order, "Lend me your key!" Once again, I replied quietly and kindly, "But tell me why, explain to me what you are going to do with it." The voice became deep and hollow and insistent; it became aggressive, "Give me your key!" I didn't answer, and as I looked at him with love and wisdom, he transformed into the devil. He got really angry and shouted at me, "Give me your key!" I remained calm and serene, steady and fearless. He calmed down and in the honeyed tones of temptation, he said, "If you lend me your key, I'll give you whatever you want." Instantaneously, I found myself in the Universe where I could see houses, addresses, different passports, luxury cars, and I felt that I could indeed have everything I wanted; there was even a beautiful, rich woman there, near an opulent house. I heard the devil continuing to tempt me, pointing out that all of my wishes, absolutely all of my wishes would be granted if I lent him my key. I replied, "But none of that is mine, I'll never take anything that doesn't belong to me." The devil got into a furious rage and he dimmed and faded away as though aspirated further away to disappear and melt into the Universe.

I found myself peacefully back before the curtain of StarLight. A brown-haired man, with a long, brown beard, wearing a mystical, sacred brown robe came toward me, looking at me in silence. The StarLight curtain opened and an ultra-modern elevator appeared. I got in with him, and, as though I knew exactly what to do, I inserted my key into the lock that started off the elevator, sending it downward. It was all very powerful and solemn. I remember as if it were yesterday. *The elevator door opened and I found myself with this man in a Library; it was Daath; the Universal Library, the Akashic Archives. The man looked at me and I intuitively understood that henceforth I had access to Daath, that for my work, I could consult and receive all the Knowledge needed to materialize in the Universe.*

It was after this dream that I began to receive multiple premonitory dreams about materialization, the stock exchange, world economy, governments, how business companies worked, etc. I only had to talk to someone during the day, or read a newspaper, watch the news, etc., and I would find myself visiting the person or situations in my dreams that night. I was also able to verify in meditation and receive lucid dreams allowing me to visit *Daath* to know what I should do. As though by magic or enchantment, symbols would appear in my mind, as indeed they still do today, after all these years.

The Angelic powers we can all attain are immeasurable, and must always respect the Divine Plan. We cannot do or have what we want in the Universe. Before setting actions and forces in motion, we have to check and verify if they are right, if they are acceptable to the Divine Plan. Furthermore, when we are on Earth, we also have to accept the role we are asked to fulfill for the good of all Humanity.

If you invoke Angels, you too will have access to these different degrees of Enlightenment, in this life or in another. But don't forget that as long as we desire and wish for spiritual powers, we cannot receive them. Ask for purity and divine qualities, and one day everything will be offered to you, in an even more beautiful way than you could ever have imagined.

Stage 4: The 7 Demons

The fourth and last Enlightenment consists in activating angelic powers related to Divine Justice. It gives us access to a universal passport enabling us to make major decisions for human destiny. Like a secret agent, it confers on us inexplicable rights for the good of the Universe, ensuring that being right at all times and in all circumstances is the founding principle of our entire being. The 4th Enlightenment is mainly related to Divine Justice, bravery, a capacity to put life plans and situations back in order. It is an integration of rigor and justice in each of our looks, emotions, actions, and even on the energy level. It leads us to discover the unexpected depth of the power of evil as educational. I didn't know this Enlightenment existed. I had experienced the other three in a state of grace and receptivity, wondering, each time, if I could possibly be any happier, I felt so fulfilled. Of course, each Enlightenment had been a long calvary, but I would go through each stage again, so convinced am I that when we are committed to Angel work and service, Up Above always guides us toward happy, beneficial evolution. The 4th Enlightenment is the final stage and it never ends. We continue to learn to live with our spiritual powers and to experiment them in divine service, both on Earth and in the Parallel Worlds.

The 4th level of Angelic Enlightenment came to me while I was unaware of its existence. I realize that we don't ask for

Enlightenments, we simply receive them when we are ready. The 4ᵗʰ one really and truly makes a secret agent of us, a very secret agent! We take part in numerous great projects in the Parallel Worlds, always to help Humanity evolve and improve. A Warrior of Light opens people's conscience and unconscious, divinely helping them discover their potential, while understanding very well that we all have to go through the ordeals we ourselves have engendered by our way of thinking, loving, and behaving in this life as well as in previous lives.

In the dream that announced this 4ᵗʰ stage of deep understanding, *I found myself facing 7 demons. They confronted me and wanted me to fight them. The atmosphere was very, very tense and dangerous; it felt as though the greatest, pitiless, machiavelian things could happen. I was insulted and told all sorts of things in order to make me angry, but I remained steadfast, not bothered or put out by them. After a while, seeing that none of their ploys destabilized me, one of the demons said to me, "You have reached an important level of mastery, but this is sure to upset you." And to my left, through a sort of plexiglass wall, I could see criminals kidnapping my daughter, forcing her to get into a car. She was screaming and crying. My whole body started shaking, and the demon said, "Come on, come and fight me! Come on, hit me and set her free. We can't upset you, we can't hurt you, so we'll get to you through your daughter!" I clenched my fists, trembling all over, and I felt such a powerful force rise within me that I could have caused the whole place to explode, it was so powerful. Shaking all over, I managed to hold myself back, declaring out loud in a solemn voice, "If that is God's Will, I accept it." And all of a sudden, the 7 demons disappeared. I knew my daughter was safe and sound, that it was all over. Great, deep peace settled in me, complete and utter trust in God's Justice, in everything that happens to us, and I began to rise up in a column of magnificent red Light. I rose and rose very intensely and found myself in a wonderful starry Sky. I felt God all around me, and I fused with His Love, Wisdom, and Absolute Justice. It was an indescribable state. After this, another scene was rapidly activated. I found myself in a sort of bedroom with a single bed. I was sitting on the floor, crouched in a corner near the bed because the energy was so powerful. The Devil was there beside me, as tall as a 120-story building. The energy was so powerful that the vibration created waves of energy, as if everything could be blown up and destroyed at any minute. The Devil spoke to me extremely forcefully, saying, "You now have great power in the Universe, but you need to mind your own business, do you understand? You're going to let me do my work! Is that clear?!"* and I woke up with this powerful Teaching that good and evil always work together, that ordeals exist, and always serve good, that they are always educational imprinted in me, inscribed in my entire being. That same night, I received another dream wherein *I saw a demon and I could see right into his very heart, the very center of his being, and I saw that he was a guide of Light, a magnificent, right being that does good, preparing ordeals and behaving evilly, diabolically so as to lead to the discovery of good.*

Now, I live my life in constant awareness that Divine Justice exists at all times, in all circumstances. I have inscribed in my very cells that whenever there is a war, or any small- or large-scale conflict, that it is educational and that it is a preparation for positive understanding one day, an opportunity for a solution, for a common agreement to be found, which will help the souls involved evolve. I now know that an evolved soul or world, is a soul or world that knows evil (hurt and wrong) and voluntarily decides not to commit it. To reach this understanding, each soul or world, has to experiment and continually vacillate between the positive and the negative until it finds its balance, its equilibrium.

Henceforth, for me, the Devil, evil, what hurts, is the *Negative* part of God. Like a father or mother, who, out of Love, sometimes send us to our room to reflect a while when we aren't right; or, when we refuse to listen, let us fly on our own wings and experiment negative aspects. The Devil is that *negative* part that tempts, stimulates, and activates in us the distorted forces that dwell in us. Evil cannot exist if we haven't engendered it ourselves by past thoughts, emotions, and behavior. We always reap what we sow. We experiment ourselves, always attracting and encountering the positive and negative aspects of ourselves. Multiple paths, illusions, and situations interact to lead us to the heart of ourselves, sooner or later.

I know, I'm aware that few books have been able to sum up in detail the work and stages of Enlightenment that all souls have to go through to become angels. The concepts that *evil is educational* and that *Divine Justice is absolute* are very profound concepts to integrate. The process of the development of conscience is full of mysteries and ambiguities in this regard. My first dreams with demons were not restful to say the least. Like an ardent knight, I fought intensely in my conscience, until one day, like a martial arts specialist who has attained the pinnacle, the acme of his art, there is no longer any need to fight, because a single look, just one understanding can set in motion all the forces of the Universe, both positive and negative.

I received permission to write this unique book. And I know in my conscience and in my soul that one day it will inspire millions of souls on Earth to discover that the true meaning of our evolution is to develop Divine Qualities, Virtues, and Powers.

CHAPTER NINE
ANGEL WORK

In this 9th and final chapter, the author, Kaya, shares his daily life with us, telling us how he materializes, makes decisions, and sets projects in motion. After years of solitary life as a hermit, just like a child, step by step, Kaya gradually learned to walk again, before teaching and testifying so that as many souls as possible may be inspired to work and activate their angelic powers on Earth.

After years of difficulties and psychological, mystical suffering, Kaya finally regained stability, discovered true spiritual happiness, and now lives a happy, beneficial life, full of love and good will, devoted to doing good. Better than anyone, he understands the extremism he went through before finding stability. He is happy to meet people from all over the world to help them integrate their heavenly capacities in peace and stability, without having to become hermits, or go into hiding to live clandestinely.

In this concluding chapter, Kaya also explains to us the origin of Angels, and work methods on how to become an angel and develop our multi-dimensional capacities.

Also included are the 3 Angel Calendars, where we can discover our 3 birth Angels with our date and time of birth; the main Qualities of the 72 Angels, and the human distortions associated with each Angel.

65. The Telephone Book

I remember the time I met Jean Morissette, our friend and first philanthropist with whom Christiane and I co-founded the international non-profit association, Universe/City Mikaël (UCM). The very first time was during the meditation reunions at the bookstore I mentioned earlier. I didn't know him; he sat on my right during the meditation and healing session. I had been told he was a lawyer so, invoking an Angel very intensely, holding his left hand, I really enjoyed myself, sending as much energy as possible, telling myself, 'We're going to make another good lawyer

on Earth ☺.' I was very intense at that time and a little extreme as I've already told you. Over time, Angelic living has taught me to calm my desire to transform people and humanity.

We spoke very little, and at that time in my life, I was very solitary and interiorized. I didn't talk much; I was more interested in observation and analysis. Two weeks after our first encounter, I had some business to sort out and I needed to consult a lawyer. Usually when I called the lawyer I'd been working with for years, he'd call me back straightaway. So, as per usual, I called his office and left a message; a few days later, I left another message, but my call was never returned. I told myself that this was a sign that I needed to find another lawyer. So I picked up the telephone book, the yellow pages, and I opened it up at the section concerning lawyers. I got down on my knees for a few minutes and I asked God to guide me to the right place, to the right lawyer. With my eyes closed, I turned to a page at random, and among the dozens of advertisements for lawyers in the region where I lived, I pointed my finger to the middle of the page to: Jean Morissette, lawyer, Sainte-Agathe-des-Monts.

As a good, obedient Angelic soldier, without knowing who he was, I called and made an appointment, and the following week I turned up at his office at the time arranged with his secretary.

On arrival, I opened the door of his office and going up the stairs I smelled a familiar odor – the same meditation incense that I used myself. Incense in a lawyer's office, I had never ever come across that before and, needless to say, I was in seventh heaven! My eyes filled with tears of gratitude to Up Above for always guiding me to the right place, at the right time. That's what I experienced, and although I have consciously experienced this guidance for the last 20 years now, each time it's as though it were the first time. I'm always deeply moved, and I thank God in silence for His Greatness, His Power. We truly live in a Living Computer, I can assure you of that. This is how all synchronicity can be so obvious, so real, and yet so magical all at the same time.

One of the partners of the firm, whom I didn't know, received me in an office and I began to explain what I needed, when suddenly, through the door that had been left ajar, I saw Jean Morissette; the very same person I had meditated with and to whom I had sent such intense energy when holding his hand in the prayer circle at the bookshop. He looked at me with a lovely smile and said, "I'm glad to see the Universe guided you here."

Years later, he became my friend, one of our first angelic students, my brother-in-law by marrying my sister Nathalie, co-founder and administrator of our non-profit foundation Universe/City Mikaël (UCM), as well as, with my sister, the father of several angel cherubs on Earth.

Hence, through dreams and signs, life guided me in each of my decisions. Whenever I arrived somewhere and met someone new who seemed to be in affinity with my Mission, I would check in my dreams that night. I have been living like this for over 20 years now and we have students, co-workers and distributors in over 43 countries throughout the world. My daughter Kasara is now a teacher, and she even helps her mother interpret her dreams. My life has become the promise that God made me when calling me to serve Him on Earth. The training was intense but it leads us to one day live a life that far surpasses all the most wonderful, longlasting happiness we could ever imagine.

66. Angels Exist Here on Earth

For those of you who would like our world to change, I can tell you that a whole movement is underway to enable angelic consciousness and angelic living to manifest more and more here on Earth. Over the last few years, we have already witnessed surprising political events in our countries, troubling revelations that have helped toward the emergence of more transparency and justice. We all see and experience this with the emergence of social networks, different forms of destabilization, economic and social difficulties, the direct consequences of the avarice and greed of the super-rich in our world, which is being more and more revealed. All of this is going on right at this very moment, as you read these lines. It is only the beginning of these re-adjustments, and none of this is coincidence. The new, recent ethical current among our public personalities, the emergence of people's deeper and deeper desire for a new, fairer, just world testify to the beginning of a new conscience for Humanity that will gradually give rise to fairer, more well-balanced leaders. A long path of awareness, reparation, change in direction and in consumer trends will have to take place before we can clearly see the resulting benefits. All of this will take time, and at times intense waves of change on the global level, in all countries, will be created.

Because, yes, we can say that our world in now on a spiritual path, undergoing complete transformation of its values and working principles. Very slowly, a new way of living, a new political, economic and social system is being prepared, and it will be based on *altruism*.

67. The Origin of Angels

The origin of the 72 Angels of The Traditional Study of Angels (Traditional Angelology) is one of the greatest mysteries dating back to the time of Moses. At the crossroads of the Babylonian, Egyptian, Greek and Roman eras, the peoples of those ancient times had many gods, each one defining different forces, different powers. Hence the Israelites established the concept of one God, represented by 72 Angels, 72 Essences, Qualities, and Powers of God. They used the Exodus to define, according to a code system of letters, the mystical combination defining the Sacred Names of the Archangels and the Angels as we know them today: Mikaël, Gabriel, etc.

In the oral Jewish and Christian tradition, it was reported that in reality the 72 Angels were the hidden treasure of the mysterious Ark of the Covenant, which was a symbolic representation of the most important secret ever revealed to Man, i.e. Knowledge of the 72 Angelic Powers. When the Jews were expelled from Jerusalem in the 1st century during the Roman Empire, this original oral Knowledge is said to have been transferred to Gerona, in Spain, where it was then written down for the very first time.

Throughout the ensuing 14 centuries, initiates who had taken refuge in the Catalan region, applied Angel work to all areas of their lives. The social and governmental structure of the community, as well as people's personal lives, were based on the Powers of the 72 Angels and on the Tree of Life.

68. The Angels' Sanctuary

The year after our wedding, I received a dream telling me we were to go to Europe. *In my dream, a sage all dressed in white, told me that Christiane and I were to go to Gerona in Spain, that we were expected there.* When I woke up, I was already thinking about when we could leave because Gerona was the place where the texts of The Traditional Study of Angels had been discovered in 1975, after remaining buried there for over 500 years since the Inquisition. A friend of ours who attended our lectures on the 72 Angels, hearing we had to go there on a Mission, very kindly offered us the plane tickets for Spain as well as a rented RV (recreational vehicle or motor home). Our trip was filled with very powerful, mystical experiences, many of which are detailed in our book entitled, *The Book of Angels, The Hidden Secrets.* One of the most important moments was the night we camped at the top of the mountain called *The Angels' Sanctuary.* I wanted to spend the night outside Gerona so as to receive any last minute information before entering the town. That night in a dream, *I saw myself arrive in Gerona town and a woman was there wearing ancient symbols; she gave me a golden key. Everything was brightly shining all around us.* On awakening, I knew that something very important was going to happen and we set off early for the town. Once we'd parked the RV, Christiane and I were very moved to be back once more in this mystical place that our souls already knew. Crossing the bridge leading to the old town, near the Call museum where the texts had been rediscovered, I felt inspired to see if we could get a tour guide – something I had never done in my whole life. At the tourist office, we booked an available private guide for 1pm. We were waiting outside when we saw the tour guide arrive and I recognized the lady who had given me the gold key in my dream. It was her; it was exactly the same woman as in my dream. Knowing through experience that people aren't necessarily aware of what we may see in dreams, or what it may mean in reality, I waited to see what would happen. She took us on a tour of the whole town, talked to us about the architecture, etc., and quite frankly, I wasn't really interested, even though it's always interesting, especially historically and symbolically. But that day, all that really interested me were the Angels and the fact that those texts had been discovered in Gerona. Seeing that she didn't really seem to be connected to us on the spiritual level,

I asked her if she knew about The Traditional Study of Angels, about the rediscovery of the texts, etc. She told us that she had only vaguely heard tell of them, and she recommended we go to the Jewish Museum in the Call; the people there would probably be able to answer my questions. Meanwhile, we went on with the guided tour, which included a visit to the Call. There I asked the old man in charge of the shop for information. I could sense his reticence and uneasiness with my question, as though the subject of Angels and Angel texts should remain unspoken, as though he were unauthorized to talk about it. He told me he had vaguely heard tell of them, and he didn't want to say anything more. I quickly felt he was hiding something, that he was following orders, so I didn't insist. We visited the library, etc., but no book referred directly to the subject apart from describing the archeological and sociological aspects of Jewish life at the time, mentioning that the Inquisition, etc., had indeed taken place here, that for more than 500 years, the buildings had been walled in and no one had had access to the site.

Once back in the town center with our tour guide, seeing that we were still wondering and not 100% satisfied with our discoveries, she told us there was a *Garden of Angels,* and asked if we'd be interested in seeing it. I was wide-eyed as a child wanting to know more, which she immediately felt and explained that she hadn't mentioned it before as there wasn't much to see there. Once we got there, Christiane and I were as happy as children who'd just discovered the greatest of treasures. There were copper plaques engraved with the names of the 72 Angels. We told the guide that we studied and worked with the Angels and that was why we had come to Gerona. She told us that the garden had been created by a Catalan poet who lived quite near Gerona. There was some sort of untold story about this garden because there had been problems in the past with the town hall but she knew nothing more about this. She asked us if we'd like to meet him, telling us that a few phonecalls would probably enable her to get his number for us. I can still see her walking in circles phoning various people until all of a sudden, she said, "I've got his number; if you like, I'll call him and see if he could possibly see you. He's very old, he must be about 84." She got through to him and he agreed to meet us the next morning at 11am at his house.

Our encounter, arranged as if by magic, was wonderful. We spent almost a whole week seeing each other every day and having meals with himself and his wife in their home. He even introduced us to architects with plans for a Cathedral for the 72 Angels. He cried when he heard Christiane's meditation CDs and the original music we were in the process of preparing to present the 72 Angels; he wanted to include them in Gerona's Garden Of Angels. When we told him that at the other end of the planet, in Canada, a School was being formed, was being built, and hundreds of people (our first students at the time) were now working, invoking the Angels in order to dream and expand their conscience, he was so moved he was full of projects and he wanted to help us. We hadn't yet begun to publish our books at that time because it was the very beginning of our lectures and we hadn't yet begun to teach outside Canada. He told us that he hadn't known that we could work with the Angels. He was sad about this because since he had found the texts, his life had been a real ordeal on the material level and he had been betrayed by several people close to him. Even remembering all of this made him very emotional because financially he had lost everything. The town council had done everything possible to expatriate him so as to recuperate the historic privilege of his discoveries for themselves. Even his friends, who had written the first texts on the subject that were circulated in France, hadn't supported him.

He explained to us in great detail that his family had descended from Jews at the time, and for generations, in their apartment they'd had a map engraved on stone, showing that there was treasure in the hidden quarter now called the Call. A very large area of the town had been walled up after the Inquisition in 1492, which had been a dreadful tragedy for their family and for many people in Gerona. Shame over what had happened had somehow made people forget these events. Today only a very general trace of what happened is kept in the Call museum, which is now linked with the University of Tel Aviv, in Israel. After being expelled, his family had kept all the texts, which was why the museum had no written documents.

When he and his close friends were children, they used to go and play in the centuries-old, long forgotten cellars, and that's how they discovered the angelic texts, which they brought home to their family. Then he went off to war during the Franco regime in Spain, and on his retirement, he decided to buy the main section of the walled up district in Gerona, there where they had found the texts, where the museum is today. In 1975 they opened a philosophical café there and his aim was to bring Jews and Christians from all over the world so they could know that the Angels were one of their greatest treasures. Thanks to him, many influential people flocked to Gerona to see these exceptional discoveries. Essentially these texts contained the Names and Qualities associated with each of the 72 Angels as well as the way They expressed Themselves, which our foundation, now publishes. At that time, the more interest grew, the more the townspeople wondered what was going to happen because in the Gerona newspapers in the 1970s, whole page headlines announced, "Millions to be invested to put Gerona on the map!" This very rapidly created a sort of jealousy and human cupidity around Tarrès and his discoveries. Enthusiastically, with childlike naivety, this man talked to everyone about it. But the promised funds failed to turn up and so he lost his entire fortune and was evicted by the town council, who used all the tricks in the book to make him leave. His friends published books that were particularly successful in France, but he remained alone and helpless in the background, with no support from them. During the week we spent together talking from morning till night, he sorrowfully told us that he hadn't known we could invoke the Angels, reciting Their Names like mantras. He had been a protector of the texts until he lost everything when he was evicted by the town council. He said to us, "I didn't work with the Angels like you. If only I'd known! I was so exalted and busy telling everyone about these texts that I worked endlessly. I now understand that it wasn't my destiny to reveal them." In spite of his great age, his white hair and mustache, this strong, solid, luminous man was very happy to hear that Angel Teaching was being reborn, that what he had accomplished would serve future generations in an updated form for the modern world, as presented by our foundation today.

One day, when our foundation has enough funds for the whole scope and extent of this project, Universe/City Mikaël (UCM) will return to Gerona to re-deposit the texts on the 72 Angels, a Treasure for Humanity and its future generations. Today, we understand that the difficult journey of The Traditional Study of Angels (Traditional Angelology) was pre-ordained by Heaven in order to preserve this Teaching, to keep it free from all dogma or religious indoctrination. Millions of people throughout the world now live according to this initiatic philosophy, which has engendered a new current of thought, a new paradigm that will undoubtedly inspire the way of living for future generations.

69. What is an Angel?

An Angel is a pure Divine State of Conscience representing Qualities, Virtues and Powers of God that we all have within us, whether we are aware of it or not. At the origin of Angels as we know them in the Christian, Jewish, and Muslim traditions, there were 72 Angels, 72 facets of the Creator with the power to lead us to discover the highest mystical states. It is a long journey, as I've shared with you, but we are here on Earth for this sole purpose. Angels are pure Energies representing our potential but most human-beings don't understand Angelic Energies well, and those who don't understand the meaning of evolution tend to make poor use of it. Hence, they distort essential aspects of the Creator, which results in human weaknesses, faults and flaws.

As defined in Traditional Angelology, each Angelic Essence bears a Hebraic name and vibration. When we pronounce the sacred Name of an Angel aloud or within ourselves, a vibratory echo is created, which acts directly on our cellular memory. Thus we are connected to Pure Divine Energies, to the Essences of Creation, which gradually activate our angelic conscience, our capacity to dream and travel in the multi-dimensions of the Universe.

Angels have always been a metaphor to express spiritual powers and the work of guide-messengers from the Parallel Worlds that, since time immemorial, have existed to help us follow our Life-Plan. They are also a symbol of what we can all become, sooner or later.

184

70. Angel Recitation (Angel Mantra)

The work to integrate an angelic conscience is basically very simple. All we have to do is to repeat the Name of an Angel like a mantra. We call it Angel Recitation (or Angel Mantra). Angel Recitation is very easy and very powerful; it can be done completely safely by adults and children alike. Standing, sitting, or lying down, we breathe naturally and repeat the Name of an Angel non-stop. We do this for as long as possible, at our own pace, within ourselves, in a low voice or out loud, (spoken, chanted, sung to a suitable melody) as often as possible throughout the day and before going to sleep. We can also do it with our child to help him fall asleep. Angel Recitation is a simple practice that can be done in all circumstances and situations in life: walking, doing sport or housework, driving, meditating, resting and relaxing, before going to sleep or on awakening, in difficult or happy times. However, we should remember that it is important to respect our own rhythm and to invoke with a sense of sacredness. The energy that has been intensified during the period of Angel Work manifests through intuitions, dreams, signs, and coincidences encountered in our daily lives. It is fascinating to see the links between the contents of our dreams and the situations in our daily lives and how they attest to the Qualities of the Angel invoked or the corresponding human distortions. Angel Recitation sets in motion or intensifies the initiatic process, and in that sense the Name of an Angel serves as a *magical formula*. Angel Work is an initiatic adventure that plunges us into the contemplation of multiple parallel realities. A wonderful way to optimize Angel Recitation is to do it while doing Angelica Meditation or Angelica Yoga exercises that are to be found in other books and CDs or mp3 downloads that our foundation publishes.

71. Our Birth Angels

At birth, each of us receives 3 Guardian Angels. Their Qualities and the corresponding human distortions indicate the strengths and weaknesses we need to work on in this life.

The first Guardian Angel corresponds to the physical level: He guides the world of action and can be identified thanks to Angel Calendar 1, according to our date of birth.

The second Guardian Angel corresponds to emotions, feelings and sentiments: He indicates the potential and virtues we need to work on, on the emotional level. His Name can be found in Angel Calendar 2, according to the day we were born.

The third Guardian Angel corresponds to the intellect and concerns the world of thoughts: He can be identified thanks to Angel Calendar 3, according to our time of birth.

As in astrology, the date and time of birth simply serve as a starting point. The goal of working with the Angelic States of Conscience consists in not only integrating the potential of our 3 Guardian Angels, but the entire Knowledge that all of the 72 Angels, all of the 72 States of God's Conscience, represent.

72. The Angel Calendars

The following pages include the 3 Angel Calendars, which allow everyone to easily identify their Guardian Angels. The first Calendar concerns the physical level, the second, the emotional level, and the third, the intellectual level.

ANGEL CALENDAR N° 1
PHYSICAL LEVEL

March 21	to	March 25	1	VEHUIAH
March 26	to	March 30	2	JELIEL
March 31	to	April 04	3	SITAEL
April 05	to	April 09	4	ELEMIAH
April 10	to	April 14	5	MAHASIAH
April 15	to	April 20	6	LELAHEL
April 21	to	April 25	7	ACHAIAH
April 26	to	April 30	8	CAHETEL
May 01	to	May 05	9	HAZIEL
May 06	to	May 10	10	ALADIAH
May 11	to	May 15	11	LAUVIAH
May 16	to	May 20	12	HAHAIAH
May 21	to	May 25	13	IEZALEL
May 26	to	May 31	14	MEBAHEL
June 01	to	June 05	15	HARIEL
June 06	to	June 10	16	HEKAMIAH
June 11	to	June 15	17	LAUVIAH
June 16	to	June 21	18	CALIEL
June 22	to	June 26	19	LEUVIAH
June 27	to	July 01	20	PAHALIAH
July 02	to	July 06	21	NELKHAEL
July 07	to	July 11	22	YEIAYEL
July 12	to	July 16	23	MELAHEL
July 17	to	July 22	24	HAHEUIAH
July 23	to	July 27	25	NITH-HAIAH
July 28	to	August 01	26	HAAIAH
August 02	to	August 06	27	YERATHEL
August 07	to	August 12	28	SEHEIAH
August 13	to	August 17	29	REIYEL
August 18	to	August 22	30	OMAEL
August 23	to	August 28	31	LECABEL
August 29	to	September 02	32	VASARIAH
September 03	to	September 07	33	YEHUIAH
September 08	to	September 12	34	LEHAHIAH
September 13	to	September 17	35	CHAVAKHIAH
September 18	to	September 23	36	MENADEL

ANGEL CALENDAR N° 1 (cont.)
PHYSICAL LEVEL

September 24	to	September 28	37	ANIEL
September 29	to	October 03	38	HAAMIAH
October 04	to	October 08	39	REHAEL
October 09	to	October 13	40	IEIAZEL
October 14	to	October 18	41	HAHAHEL
October 19	to	October 23	42	MIKAËL
October 24	to	October 28	43	VEULIAH
October 29	to	November 02	44	YELAHIAH
November 03	to	November 07	45	SEALIAH
November 08	to	November 12	46	ARIEL
November 13	to	November 17	47	ASALIAH
November 18	to	November 22	48	MIHAEL
November 23	to	November 27	49	VEHUEL
November 28	to	December 02	50	DANIEL
December 03	to	December 07	51	HAHASIAH
December 08	to	December 12	52	IMAMIAH
December 13	to	December 16	53	NANAEL
December 17	to	December 21	54	NITHAEL
December 22	to	December 26	55	MEBAHIAH
December 27	to	December 31	56	POYEL
January 01	to	January 05	57	NEMAMIAH
January 06	to	January 10	58	YEIALEL
January 11	to	January 15	59	HARAHEL
January 16	to	January 20	60	MITZRAEL
January 21	to	January 25	61	UMABEL
January 26	to	January 30	62	IAHHEL
January 31	to	February 04	63	ANAUEL
February 05	to	February 09	64	MEHIEL
February 10	to	February 14	65	DAMABIAH
February 15	to	February 19	66	MANAKEL
February 20	to	February 24	67	EYAEL
February 25	to	February 29	68	HABUHIAH
March 01	to	March 05	69	ROCHEL
March 06	to	March 10	70	JABAMIAH
March 11	to	March 15	71	HAIAIEL
March 16	to	March 20	72	MUMIAH

ANGEL CALENDAR N° 2
EMOTIONAL LEVEL

JAN.	FEB.	MARCH	APRIL	MAY	JUNE
1: #65	1: #25	1: #53	1: #12	1: #41	1: #71
2: #66	2: #26	2: #54	2: #13	2: #42	2: #72
3: #67	3: #27	3: #55	3: #14	3: #43	3: #1
4: #68	4: #28	4: #56	4: #15	4: #44	4: #2
5: #69	5: #29	5: #57	5: #16	5: #45	5: #3
6: #70	6: #30	6: #58	6: #17	6: #46	6: #4
7: #71	7: #31	7: #59	7: #18	7: #47	7: #5
8: #72	8: #32	8: #60	8: #19	8: #48	8: #6
9: #1	9: #33	9: #61	9: #20	9: #49	9: #7
10: #2	10: #34	10: #62	10: #21	10: #50	10: #8
11: #3	11: #35	11: #63	11: #22	11: #51	11: #9
12: #4	12: #36	12: #64	12: #23	12: #52	12: #10
13: #5	13: #37	13: #65	13: #24	13: #53	13: *
14: #6	14: #38	14: #66	14: #25	14: #54	14: #11
15: #7	15: #39	15: #67	15: #26	15: #55	15: #12
16: #8	16: #40	16: #68	16: #27	16: #56	16: #13
17: #9	17: #41	17: #69	17: *	17: #57	17: #14
18: #10	18: #42	18: #70	18: #28	18: #58	18: #15
19: #11	19: #43	19: #71	19: #29	19: #59	19: #16
20: #12	20: #44	20: #72	20: #30	20: *	20: #17
21: #13	21: #45	21: #1	21: #31	21: #60	21: #18
22: #14	22: #46	22: #2	22: #32	22: #61	22: #19
23: #15	23: #47	23: #3	23: #33	23: #62	23: #20
24: #16/17	24: #48	24: #4	24: #34	24: #63	24: #21
25: #18	25: #49	25: #5	25: #35	25: #64	25: #22
26: #19	26: #50	26: #6	26: #36	26: #65	26: #23
27: #20	27: #51	27: #7	27: #37	27: #66	27: #24
28: #21	28: #52	28: #8	28: #38	28: #67	28: #25
29: #22	29: #52	29: #9	29: #39	29: #68	29: #26
30: #23		30: #10	30: #40	30: #69	30: #27
31: #24		31: #11		31: #70	

How to find your Guardian Angel on the emotional level:
Note the figure to the right of your date of birth on this Calendar. This is your Guardian Angel. All you have to do is to consult Angel Calendar No. 1 to find this Angel's name. Particularities: 1) * on the indicated day, from midnight to noon, the Angel of the preceding day presides, and from noon to midnight, the Angel of the following day presides. E.g., Angel 27 YERATHEL presides on April 16, and on the 17th until noon,

ANGEL CALENDAR N° 2 (cont.)
EMOTIONAL LEVEL

JULY	AUG.	SEPT.	OCT.	NOV.	DEC.
1: #28	1: #57	1: #15	1: #44	1: #3	1: #33
2: #29	2: #58	2: #16	2: #45	2: #4	2: #34
3: #30	3: #59	3: #17	3: #46	3: #5	3: #35
4: #31	4: #60	4: #18	4: #47	4: #6	4: #36
5: *	5: #61	5: #19	5: #48	5: #7	5: #37
6: #32	6: #62	6: #20	6: #49	6: #8	6: #38
7: #33	7: #63	7: #21	7: #50	7: #9	7: #39
8: #34	8: #64	8: #22	8: #51	8: #10	8: #40
9: #35	9: #65	9: #23	9: #52	9: #11	9: #41
10: #36	10: #66	10: #24	10: #53	10: #12	10: #42
11: #37	11: #67	11: #25	11: #54	11: #13	11: #43
12: #38	12: #68	12: #26	12: #55	12: #14	12: #44
13: #39	13: #69	13: #27	13: #56	13: #15	13: #45
14: #40	14: #70	14: #28	14: #57	14: #16	14: #46
15: #41	15: #71	15: #29	15: #58	15: #17	15: #47
16: #42	16: #72	16: #30	16: #59	16: #18	16: #48
17: #43	17: #1	17: #31	17: #60	17: #19	17: #49
18: #44	18: #2	18: #32	18: #61	18: #20	18: #50
19: #45	19: *	19: #33	19: #62	19: #21	19: #51
20: #46	20: #3	20: #34	20: #63	20: #22	20: #52
21: #47	21: #4	21: *	21: #64	21: #23	21: #53
22: #48	22: #5	22: #35	22: #65	22: #24	22: #54
23: #49	23: #6	23: #36	23: #66	23: #25	23: #55
24: #50	24: #7	24: #37	24: #67	24: #26	24: #56
25: #51	25: #8	25: #38	25: #68	25: #27	25: #57
26: *	26: #9	26: #39	26: #69	26: #28	26: #58
27: #52	27: #10	27: #40	27: #70	27: #29	27: #59/60
28: #53	28: #11	28: #41	28: #71	28: #30	28: #61
29: #54	29: #12	29: #42	29: #72	29: #31	29: #62
30: #55	30: #13	30: #43	30: #1	30: #32	30: #63
31: #56	31: #14		31: #2		31: #64

and the following Angel 28 SEHEIAH presides on April 17 afternoon, and on April 18. 2) January 24 is governed by two Angels: Angel 16 HEKAMIAH from midnight to 6 pm and Angel 17 LAUVIAH from 6 pm to midnight. Likewise on December 27, there are two Angels: Angel 59 HARAHEL from midnight to 6 pm and Angel 60 MITZRAEL from 6 pm to midnight.

ANGEL CALENDAR N° 3
INTELLECTUAL LEVEL

Midnight	to	0:19	am	1	VEHUIAH
0:20	to	0:39	am	2	JELIEL
0:40	to	0:59	am	3	SITAEL
1:00	to	1:19	am	4	ELEMIAH
1:20	to	1:39	am	5	MAHASIAH
1:40	to	1:59	am	6	LELAHEL
2:00	to	2:19	am	7	ACHAIAH
2:20	to	2:39	am	8	CAHETEL
2:40	to	2:59	am	9	HAZIEL
3:00	to	3:19	am	10	ALADIAH
3:20	to	3:39	am	11	LAUVIAH
3:40	to	3:59	am	12	HAHAIAH
4:00	to	4:19	am	13	IEZALEL
4:20	to	4:39	am	14	MEBAHEL
4:40	to	4:59	am	15	HARIEL
5:00	to	5:19	am	16	HEKAMIAH
5:20	to	5:39	am	17	LAUVIAH
5:40	to	5:59	am	18	CALIEL
6:00	to	6:19	am	19	LEUVIAH
6:20	to	6:39	am	20	PAHALIAH
6:40	to	6:59	am	21	NELKHAEL
7:00	to	7:19	am	22	YEIAYEL
7:20	to	7:39	am	23	MELAHEL
7:40	to	7:59	am	24	HAHEUIAH
8:00	to	8:19	am	25	NITH-HAIAH
8:20	to	8:39	am	26	HAAIAH
8:40	to	8:59	am	27	YERATHEL
9:00	to	9:19	am	28	SEHEIAH
9:20	to	9:39	am	29	REIYEL
9:40	to	9:59	am	30	OMAEL
10:00	to	10:19	am	31	LECABEL
10:20	to	10:39	am	32	VASARIAH
10:40	to	10:59	am	33	YEHUIAH
11:00	to	11:19	am	34	LEHAHIAH
11:20	to	11:39	am	35	CHAVAKHIAH
11:40	to	11:59	am	36	MENADEL

ANGEL CALENDAR N° 3 (cont.)
INTELLECTUAL LEVEL

Noon	to	12:19	pm	37	ANIEL
12:20	to	12:39	pm	38	HAAMIAH
12:40	to	12:59	pm	39	REHAEL
13:00	to	13:19	pm	40	IEIAZEL
13:20	to	13:39	pm	41	HAHAHEL
13:40	to	13:59	pm	42	MIKAËL
14:00	to	14:19	pm	43	VEULIAH
14:20	to	14:39	pm	44	YELAHIAH
14:40	to	14:59	pm	45	SEALIAH
15:00	to	15:19	pm	46	ARIEL
15:20	to	15:39	pm	47	ASALIAH
15:40	to	15:59	pm	48	MIHAEL
16:00	to	16:19	pm	49	VEHUEL
16:20	to	16:39	pm	50	DANIEL
16:40	to	16:59	pm	51	HAHASIAH
17:00	to	17:19	pm	52	IMAMIAH
17:20	to	17:39	pm	53	NANAEL
17:40	to	17:59	pm	54	NITHAEL
18:00	to	18:19	pm	55	MEBAHIAH
18:20	to	18:39	pm	56	POYEL
18:40	to	18:59	pm	57	NEMAMIAH
19:00	to	19:19	pm	58	YEIALEL
19:20	to	19:39	pm	59	HARAHEL
19:40	to	19:59	pm	60	MITZRAEL
20:00	to	20:19	pm	61	UMABEL
20:20	to	20:39	pm	62	IAHHEL
20:40	to	20:59	pm	63	ANAUEL
21:00	to	21:19	pm	64	MEHIEL
21:20	to	21:39	pm	65	DAMABIAH
21:40	to	21:59	pm	66	MANAKEL
22:00	to	22:19	pm	67	EYAEL
22:20	to	22:39	pm	68	HABUHIAH
22:40	to	22:59	pm	69	ROCHEL
23:00	to	23:19	pm	70	JABAMIAH
23:20	to	23:39	pm	71	HAIAIEL
23:40	to	23:59	pm	72	MUMIAH

73. Angel Work

When carried out on a daily basis, Angel Work creates a gradual opening of our subconscious and unconscious, which manifests in several ways:

1) As explained, in the beginning, **our souls states (moods) go from one extreme to another,** e.g. from wonderful well-being to deep anxiety;

2) **The sharpness of our five senses (sight, hearing, smell, taste and touch) is considerably increased** and we gradually develop clairvoyance, clairaudience and clairsentience;

3) **The frequency and intensity of our dreams are gradually increased** and we can better interpret them by associating them with the Angelic State of Conscience invoked. If we don't yet dream, after only a few weeks of diligent Angel Recitation, dreams are set off. Thus, for all those who invoke the Angels, the interpretation of dreams and daily signs engenders deep, mystical experiences. We acquire great spiritual autonomy, because the study of signs and dreams allows us to gradually learn the various steps and stages of our initiatic journey.

THE QUALITIES
OF THE 72 ANGELS

1	**Vehuiah**	Divine Will
2	**Jeliel**	Love, Wisdom
3	**Sitael**	Construction
4	**Elemiah**	Divine Power
5	**Mahasiah**	Rectifying errors before they materialize
6	**Lelahel**	Divine Light that heals everything (Light of Love)
7	**Achaiah**	Patience
8	**Cahetel**	Divine Blessing
9	**Haziel**	Universal Love
10	**Aladiah**	Second chance
11	**Lauviah**	Victory
12	**Hahaiah**	Refuge, meditation, interiorization
13	**Iezalel**	Fidelity
14	**Mebahel**	Commitment
15	**Hariel**	Purification
16	**Hekamiah**	Loyalty to Divine Principles
17	**Lauviah**	Revelations
18	**Caliel**	Truth
19	**Leuviah**	Intelligence
20	**Pahaliah**	Deliverance
21	**Nelkhael**	Facilitates learning
22	**Yeiayel**	Renown, fame
23	**Melahel**	Capacity to heal, healthy food
24	**Haheuiah**	Protection
25	**Nith-Haiah**	Bearer of Supreme Wisdom and Love
26	**Haahiah**	Discretion
27	**Yerathel**	Confidence
28	**Seheiah**	Foresight
29	**Reiyel**	Liberation
30	**Omael**	Multiplication, joy
31	**Lecabel**	Talent for solving the enigmas of life
32	**Vasariah**	Clemency, makes it easy to forgive
33	**Yehuiah**	Subordination, listens to what is good, what is right
34	**Lehahiah**	Obedience
35	**Chavakhiah**	Reconciliation, family
36	**Menadel**	Work

THE QUALITIES (cont.)
OF THE 72 ANGELS

37	ANIEL	Helps change bad habits and old, erroneous structures
38	HAAMIAH	Sense of rituals and preparations
39	REHAEL	Submission, receptivity
40	IEIAZEL	Consolation, comfort
41	HAHAHEL	Mission
42	MIKAËL	Political order
43	VEULIAH	Prosperity
44	YELAHIAH	Warrior of Light
45	SEALIAH	Motivation
46	ARIEL	Revelatory perception, psychic abilities
47	ASALIAH	Contemplation
48	MIHAEL	Fertility, marriage
49	VEHUEL	Elevation towards Greatness and Wisdom
50	DANIEL	Eloquence, helps to speak well
51	HAHASIAH	Universal Medicine
52	IMAMIAH	Makes it easy to recognize our mistakes, our misactions
53	NANAEL	Spiritual communication
54	NITHAEL	Eternal youth
55	MEBAHIAH	Intellectual clarity
56	POYEL	Fortune, support and wealth
57	NEMAMIAH	Discernment, discovers and does what is right
58	YEIALEL	Mental power
59	HARAHEL	Intellectual abundance
60	MITZRAEL	Reparation
61	UMABEL	Friendship, affinity
62	IAHHEL	Knowledge re-discovered
63	ANAUEL	Perception of Unity, inner well-being
64	MEHIEL	Invigoration, inspiration
65	DAMABIAH	Fountain of Wisdom, purity
66	MANAKEL	Knowledge of good and evil
67	EYAEL	Sublimation, metamorphosis, change
68	HABUHIAH	Healing
69	ROCHEL	Restitution, helps find what we've lost
70	JABAMIAH	Alchemy, transforms evil into good
71	HAIAIEL	Divine arms, inner strength
72	MUMIAH	Rebirth, loves life

THE ASSOCIATED HUMAN DISTORTIONS, FLAWS AND WEAKNESSES

1	VEHUIAH	Imposes one's will, forces Destiny, unmotivated
2	JELIEL	Lack of love and wisdom
3	SITAEL	Destruction
4	ELEMIAH	Manipulation to satisfy personal needs
5	MAHASIAH	Tendency to want revenge, holds a grudge
6	LELAHEL	Ambition
7	ACHAIAH	Impatience
8	CAHETEL	Only think about ourselves, selfishness
9	HAZIEL	Lack of love; possessive, jealous, fear of loving and being loved
10	ALADIAH	Witchery, waste
11	LAUVIAH	Failure, jealousy, pride
12	HAHAIAH	Isolation, flees others
13	IEZALEL	Infidelity, doesn't keep promises
14	MEBAHEL	Detachment, pushes others away
15	HARIEL	Blames others
16	HEKAMIAH	Treachery, war, rebellion
17	LAUVIAH	Sadness
18	CALIEL	Lies
19	LEUVIAH	Loss of our intellectual faculties, memory problems
20	PAHALIAH	Abuse and waste, fanaticism, exploits others
21	NELKHAEL	Learning difficulties, difficult exams
22	YEIAYEL	Profiteer, wants to be acknowledged
23	MELAHEL	Illness, artificial food
24	HAHEUIAH	Lacks protection
25	NITH-HAIAH	Black magic, witchery
26	HAAHIAH	Indiscretion, selfishness, family problems
27	YERATHEL	Hyperactivity, lack of confidence
28	SEHEIAH	Carelessness, deep anxiety
29	REIYEL	Limiting situation, prison
30	OMAEL	Lack of success, repeated failure
31	LECABEL	Manipulates and exploits others
32	VASARIAH	Vengeance
33	YEHUIAH	Rebellion, aggressiveness, doesn't listen
34	LEHAHIAH	Disobedience
35	CHAVAKHIAH	Family problems
36	MENADEL	Doesn't want to work, laziness

THE ASSOCIATED HUMAN DISTORTIONS, FLAWS AND WEAKNESSES (cont.)

37	ANIEL	Refuses to change
38	HAAMIAH	Impoliteness, lacks preparation
39	REHAEL	Doesn't accept authority
40	IEIAZEL	Dependencies, despondent
41	HAHAHEL	Seeks to convince
42	MIKAËL	Disorder
43	VEULIAH	Only thinks about money
44	YELAHIAH	Fanatic, terrorist
45	SEALIAH	Lack of motivation and enthusiasm
46	ARIEL	Lacks intuition
47	ASALIAH	Panics, doesn't understand
48	MIHAEL	Separation, divorce, jealousy
49	VEHUEL	Humiliates others
50	DANIEL	Has difficulty speaking
51	HAHASIAH	Doesn't understand illness
52	IMAMIAH	Doesn't acknowledge his mistakes, love problems
53	NANAEL	Refuses spiritual knowledge
54	NITHAEL	Seduction
55	MEBAHIAH	Lacks ideas
56	POYEL	Poverty
57	NEMAMIAH	An intellect without principles, bad ideas
58	YEIALEL	Craftiness, imposes his ideas
59	HARAHEL	Intellectual difficulties
60	MITZRAEL	Doesn't want to repair
61	UMABEL	Has difficulty making friends
62	IAHHEL	Refuses to learn
63	ANAUEL	Feels alone and separate from others
64	MEHIEL	Lacks inspiration, critical
65	DAMABIAH	Emotional problems
66	MANAKEL	Doesn't understand good and evil
67	EYAEL	Fear of change
68	HABUHIAH	Illness
69	ROCHEL	Taking what doesn't belong to us
70	JABAMIAH	Blockage, remains stuck in a problem
71	HAIAIEL	Terrorist, war, quarrels
72	MUMIAH	Suicide, difficulty finishing what we have started, doesn't like life

74. Angel Work in the Family

Since its foundation in 2001, the non-profit organization Universe/City Mikaël (UCM) now has over 450 volunteers from all over the world who actively participate in diffusing and translating Angelic Knowledge in numerous countries. For several years now, hundreds and thousands of people have already been working on becoming Angels on Earth. Just as I did, they too go through intense, daily initiations which transform them. Several teachers now work with us, teaching how to develop our Angelic potential. Recently we also founded *Angelica Pratica Clinic*, a therapeutic treatment clinic, with Dr. François Bouchard and his wife, Denise Fredette, who give holistic treatments using Angel Work and symbolic language. Our work and books are published in more than 43 countries throughout the world, and continue to reach more and more new souls, new initiates in the making. Our foundation is also specialized in symbolic language and several reference books on the interpretation of dreams, signs, and symbols have been published, as well as the webinars, lectures, workshops, seminars, and training courses for therapists and future teachers that we organize throughout the year in several countries. For more information, you are welcome to visit our Internet websites: **www.ucm.in**.

Moreover, my wife Christiane and I have the additional happiness of sharing this Angelic Mission on Earth with our daughter Kasara and our future son-in-law, Anthony, who also inspire and teach the benefits of angelic living on Earth.

75. Our Message: YOU CAN BECOME AN ANGEL

The essence of our Mission on Earth is to make known the true meaning of what an Angel is. Very often Angels are represented in a very light-hearted, airy-fairy way as though They belonged to La-La land, while, in actual fact, They are the Keys to Universal Consciousness. Our goal is to help people of all nations, races, and religions to discover the meaning of Life and the reason why we have come to Earth: we are here on Earth to become Angels.

BECOMING AN ANGEL
TABLE OF CONTENTS

⦿UCM

www.ucm.ca
org@ucm.ca

AVAILABLE FROM OUR PUBLISHING HOUSE

BECOMING AN ANGEL
THE PATH TO ENLIGHTENMENT
AUTOBIOGRAPHY
Kaya
ISBN: 978-2-923654-67-6

THE BOOK OF ANGELS
THE HIDDEN SECRETS
THE TRADITIONAL STUDY OF ANGELS
Kaya and Christiane Muller
ISBN: 978-2-923097-54-1

DICTIONARY
DREAMS-SIGNS-SYMBOLS
THE SOURCE CODE
Kaya and Christiane Muller
ISBN: 978-2-923654-25-6

ANGELICA YOGA
INTRODUCTION
Kaya and Christiane Muller
ISBN: 978-2-923097-63-3

THE SPIRITUAL DIARY OF A NINE-YEAR-OLD CHILD
Kasara
ISBN: 978-2-923097-66-4

**HOW TO INTERPRET
DREAMS & SIGNS**
Kaya
ISBN: 978-2-923654-11-9

THE 72 ANGEL CARDS
DREAMS, SIGNS, MEDITATION
Kaya and Christiane Muller
ISBN: 978-2-923097-60-2

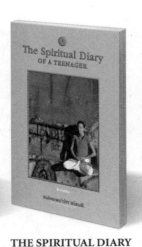

HOW TO READ SIGNS
THE ORIGIN OF ANGELS,
SIGNS & SYMBOLS
Kaya and Christiane Muller
ISBN: 978-2-923097-61-9

**THE SPIRITUAL DIARY
OF A TEENAGER**
Kasara
e-book: 978-2-923654-08-9

**IN THE LAND
OF BLUE SKIES**
Gabriell, Kaya
and Christiane Muller
ISBN: 978-2-923097-65-7

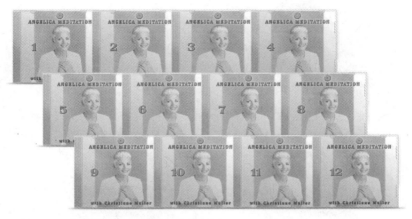

ANGELICA MEDITATION COLLECTION

CD 1: (Angels 72 to 67)   CD 5: (Angels 48 to 43)   CD 9: (Angels 24 to 19)
CD 2: (Angels 66 to 61)   CD 6: (Angels 42 to 37)   CD 10: (Angels 18 to 13)
CD 3: (Angels 60 to 55)   CD 7: (Angels 36 to 31)   CD 11: (Angels 12 to 7)
CD 4: (Angels 54 to 49)   CD 8: (Angels 30 to 25)   CD 12: (Angels 6 to 1)

ANGELICA MUSICA COLLECTION

CD 1: (Angels 72 to 67)   CD 5: (Angels 48 to 43)   CD 9: (Angels 24 to 19)
CD 2: (Angels 66 to 61)   CD 6: (Angels 42 to 37)   CD 10: (Angels 18 to 13)
CD 3: (Angels 60 to 55)   CD 7: (Angels 36 to 31)   CD 11: (Angels 12 to 7)
CD 4: (Angels 54 to 49)   CD 8: (Angels 30 to 25)   CD 12: (Angels 6 to 1)

BORN UNDER THE STAR OF CHANGE
Kaya
Production: Russ DeSalvo, New York, USA
Record Label: Golden Wisdom Records / Airgo Music
Genre: Adult Contemporary / Pop / Inspirational
Format: CD and MP3
# of songs: 13
Item number: 627843159308

ANGELICA MANTRA VOL. 1
ANGELS 1 to 12
Kasara

ANGELICA MANTRA VOL. 2
ANGELS 13 to 24
Kasara

ANGELICA MANTRA VOL. 3
ANGELS 25 to 36
Kasara

ANGELICA MANTRA VOL. 4
ANGELS 37 to 48
Kasara

GREETING CARDS
EXPOSITION ANGELICA
Artist: Gabriell
A collection of 65 greeting cards

NOTES

NOTES

NOTES

NOTES

NOTES

NOTES

NOTES

NOTES

NOTES

NOTES